Approaches to Data Design, Engineering, and Development

IDMA 202 COURSE STUDY GUIDE

Insurance Data Management Association (IDMA) Associate Insurance Data Manager (AIDM) Designation Program

Technics Publications
SEDONA, ARIZONA

Published by:

115 Linda Vista
Sedona, AZ 86336 USA
www.TechnicsPub.com

Cover design by Lorena Molinari

First Edition

First Printing 2026

Copyright © 2026 Insurance Data Management Association, Inc. (IDMA)

ISBN, print ed.   9798898161101
ISBN, Kindle ed.   9798898161118
ISBN, PDF ed.   9798898161125

Library of Congress Control Number: 2026940449

Contents

Introduction

Founded in 1983, IDMA is an independent nonprofit professional association dedicated to increasing the level of professionalism, knowledge, and visibility of insurance data management through education, research, annual forums, local chapter meetings, news bulletins, and peer-to-peer networking. It serves individuals employed in any aspect of insurance data management. This includes individuals engaged in any of the following enterprise information governance activities within various functional areas of insurance companies, regulatory bodies, statistical/rating organizations, industry consulting firms, professional associations and learned societies, and technology research and services providers:

- data definition
- data collection
- data administration
- data standards
- data processing
- data analysis
- internal and external data reporting
- data quality.

The main objective of IDMA is the administration of an educational program designed to increase professional proficiency and to provide a professional designation in the data management discipline. Additionally, IDMA provides an ongoing forum for the discussion of issues and innovations in data management through technical seminars, educational workshops, and publications.

IDMA courses, workshops, and forums are highly recommended for a broad audience including new hires, IT and data modeling professionals who want to broaden their knowledge of the business side of insurance data management, anyone who manages and governs data in the industry (statistical, or management information data), and anyone who needs to use or communicate good quality data/information – from actuaries to underwriters, and claims and analytics professionals.

Students who complete the four IDMA-developed courses and successfully pass the examinations are awarded an *Associate Insurance Data Manager (AIDM®)* designation. The IDMA courses may be taken in any order; there are no prerequisites. However, the courses are numbered to indicate a recommended sequence.

Students who complete additional course work from other selected insurance industry educational organizations and successfully pass the specified examinations receive the *Certified Insurance Data Manager (CIDM®)* designation.

For details on the designation requirements, please refer to the IDMA website at www.IDMA.org or call our office at +1 (201) 469-3069.

Using this Course Guide

This course guide will help you learn the course content and prepare for the exam.

Almost all assignments in this course guide, except for the final assignment, which is a recap of the prior assignments, include the following components:

- **Educational Objectives**. These are the most important study tools in the course guide. Because all of the questions on the exam are based on the Educational Objectives, the best way to study for the exam is to focus on these objectives.

- **Key Terms and Concepts**. These terms and concepts are fundamental to understanding the assignment. After completing the required reading, test your understanding of the assignment's Key Terms and Concepts by writing their definitions.

- **Review Questions**. The review questions test your understanding of what you have read. Review the Educational Objectives and required reading, then answer the questions to the best of your ability. When you are finished, check the answers at the end of the assignment to evaluate your comprehension.

- **Discussion Questions**. These questions are intended to continue to test your knowledge of the required reading by applying what you've studied to real-life situations. No suggested answers are provided at the end of the assignment for these types of open discussion questions. Answers may vary by student and will depend on their organization's culture, resources, and processes.

Important Note Applicable to All IDMA Course Material: IDMA strives to keep all of its course material current. The information provided is up to date at the time of publication. The timing and pace of industry changes, along with the constraints of publication, can at times result in a lag in updates being included. IDMA regularly reviews content to ensure that it is current and will publish updates as necessary and appropriate.

Exam Information

IDMA exams are given online, consist of 100 multiple-choice and true/false type questions, and are three hours long. Unofficial scores are tabulated and issued immediately after the exam completion. Official scores are mailed to students within 15 business days after the conclusion of the exam cycle. The passing score is 70%.

Students are allowed to take more than one course exam during an exam cycle. Students are also allowed to retake an exam within the same exam cycle if they were not successful on their first try.

Exams are conducted with no reference materials, papers, books, or other aids permitted in the room. No student may communicate with another during the exam. Students are not allowed to maintain copies of their exams. All exam materials are considered the property of IDMA.

Exam Registration Information and Requirements

Currently, IDMA does not contract with testing centers (such as Prometric, Pearson, and Kryterion) to host its exams onsite. IDMA exams are given, so far as possible, at the student's worksite with the cooperation of the human resources or education department in locating a proctor and site.

NOTE: Students are responsible for locating a proctor and providing IDMA with the proctor's contact information. A proctor could be anyone from your HR department, your manager, or a staffer. A week before the exam, IDMA will email your proctor a "proctor package" that explains the exam process. You will also receive your exam pass via email around the same time.

The purchase of the study guide for the current IDMA course does not automatically register a candidate for the examination. As you proceed with your studies, be sure to arrange for your exam.

- Visit our website at www.IDMA.org to access and print the exam registration form, which contains information and forms needed to register for your exam.
- Plan to register with IDMA well in advance of your exam. Late fees apply two weeks prior to the start of the exam cycle.
- Coordinate with your proctor on the exam date and start time.

How to Study for IDMA Exams

Use the assigned study materials (textbook and course guide). Focus your study on the Educational Objectives presented at the beginning of each course guide assignment. Thoroughly read the textbook and any other assigned materials, and then complete the course guide exercises. Choose a study method that best suits your needs; for example, participate in a traditional class, an informal study group, or study on your own. IDMA recommends that you begin your studies for the exam at least two months before your scheduled exam date.

Student Resources

For more information on any of the IDMA publications, course examinations, and other services:

- Visit our website at www.IDMA.org.
- Call us at +1 (201) 469-3069.

- Fax us at +1 (201) 748-1690.
- Write to us at Insurance Data Management Association (IDMA), 545 Washington Boulevard, 16th Floor, Jersey City, NJ 07310.

Introduction to Data Management in the Insurance Industry

Educational Objectives

Upon completion of this assignment, you should be able to:

1. Define data, information, and knowledge. Describe the relationship between them.
2. Describe how the insurance product differs from other products.
3. Describe how this difference affects an insurance company's need for information.
4. Describe how outside influences affect the pricing of insurance products and insurers' need for data and information.
5. Describe how data helps insurers manage the policy life cycle.
6. Explain how managing all of an insurance company's data provides a competitive advantage.
7. Identify the trends in the insurance industry that led to the emergence of data management as a distinct profession within the insurance industry.
8. Describe the roles insurance data managers play for various disciplines in the insurance industry.
9. Identify the founding purpose of IDMA and describe its role in the insurance industry.
10. Identify the role IDMA plays in developing and promoting professional standards for insurance data managers.
11. Outline the four Commitments in the Standards of Professionalism for Insurance Data Managers.

For each assignment, define or describe each of the Key Terms and Concepts and answer each of the Review and Discussion Questions.

Key Terms and Concepts

Agents:

Brokers:

Direct writers:

Endorsement(s):

Exclusive agents:

File-and-Use laws:

Flex-rating laws:

Independent agents:

Law of large numbers:

National Association of Insurance Commissioners (NAIC):

Open competition laws:

Prior Approval Laws:

Policy period:

Rider(s):

Statistical agents:

Statistical plans:

Usage-based insurance (UBI) or Pay-as-You-Drive rating plans:

Review Question

1) Define the differences among data, information, and knowledge, and describe their relationships.

Discussion Questions

NOTE: The questions below are intended to continue to challenge you to test your knowledge of the required reading by applying what you have studied to real-life situations.

No suggested answers are provided at the end of the assignment for these types of open discussion questions. Answers may vary by student and will depend on their organization's culture, resources, and processes.

1) Discuss a real-life example of the 1-10-100 Rule.

2) How does your company handle all the unstructured data?

3) Discuss some of the methods you or your colleagues have used to decide or come to a conclusion when information has been insufficient, inaccurate, poorly presented, outdated, or untimely.

Answers to Assignment 1 Questions

NOTE: These answers are provided to give students a basic understanding of acceptable types of responses. They are often not the only valid answers and are not intended to provide an exhaustive response to the questions.

Key Terms and Concepts

Agents: Representatives of insurers and they can be exclusive agents, direct writers, or independent agents.

Brokers: Represent applicants and insureds in their dealings with insurance companies.

Direct writers: Direct writers are insurers that do not use any agents or brokers but write business directly with the insured.

Endorsement(s): Changes to a policy contract are generally made by adding forms referred to as endorsements.

Exclusive agents: Exclusive agents are contracted to represent a single insurer.

File-and-Use laws: In jurisdictions with prior approval laws for a line of insurance, insurers are required to file rates with state regulators, but may use them prior to receiving regulatory approval. An alternative to file-and-use laws is flex-rating laws.

Flex-rating laws: In jurisdictions with prior-approval laws for a line of insurance, insurers must file new rates but may put them into effect before approval, provided the new rates are not more than a specified percentage above or below the existing rates.

Independent agents: Represent several insurance companies and are employees of an agency rather than an insurer.

Law of large numbers: The law of large numbers essentially states that larger and more consistent statistical samples have a greater probability of producing accurate predictions than smaller samples.

National Association of Insurance Commissioners (NAIC): An association comprising of insurance regulators from the 50 states, the District of Columbia, and the four U.S. territories to provide a forum for the development of uniform standards and policies where uniformity is appropriate.

Open competition laws: In jurisdictions with prior approval laws for a line of insurance, insurers are not required to file rates with the state insurance department.

Policy period: A policy period may be a year, but it can be shorter or longer.

Prior Approval Laws: In jurisdictions with prior approval laws for a line of insurance, insurers must submit new rates and rate changes to regulators and obtain approval of those rates before implementing them.

Rider(s): In the case of life and health insurance policies, changes to a policy contract are generally referred to as riders.

Statistical agents: State insurance departments designated agents to collect specific data.

Statistical plans: Statistical agents develop statistical plans that define the specific data insurers are to provide, the way in which insurers are to code and submit the data, and when they are to be submitted.

Usage-based insurance (UBI) or Pay-as-You-Drive rating plans: Insurers are using automobile event data recorders (EDR), sometimes called telematics or "black boxes", and smartphones to monitor insureds' mileage, speed, or other driving behaviors so as to provide usage-based insurance (UBI) or pay-as-you-drive rating plans.

Review Question

1) **Define the differences among data, information, and knowledge, and describe their relationships.**

Data is the raw material. It is the individual facts, numbers, codes, dates, names, transactions, or observations that have been collected but may not mean much by themselves. For example, a policy number, a claim date, a premium amount, or a ZIP code are all pieces of data. They are useful, but only after someone organizes them and understands what they are connected to.

Information is data that has been organized so it has meaning. Once data is sorted, compared, summarized, or placed in context, it starts to answer questions. For example, a list of individual claims is data, but a report showing claim trends by territory or type of policy is information. The textbook explains that insurers need large volumes of data and information to make good business decisions, price products, manage policies, meet reporting requirements, and gain a competitive advantage.

Knowledge goes one step further. It is the understanding gained from using information, experience, and judgment to make decisions. In other words, data becomes information when it is given context, and information becomes knowledge when people understand what it means and how to act on it. Their relationship is like a ladder. Data is the starting point, information gives it meaning, and knowledge helps a business decide what to do next.

Insurance Data and Information

Educational Objectives

Upon completion of this assignment, you should be able to:

1. Describe the types of information collected by insurers to support their operations.
2. Identify sources of information that insurers use.
3. Describe why insurers use external information.
4. Describe the considerations involved in using different sources of information.
5. Define the rating variable and give examples for different lines of insurance.
6. Describe how insurance companies use premium and loss information to monitor their operations.
7. Describe different methods of aggregating premium and loss data.
8. Identify the advantages and disadvantages of each data aggregation method.
9. Define the concepts of dynamic data and persistent data.
10. Define Personally Identifiable Information (PII) and describe the rationale for the regulation of its use and disclosure.
11. Describe the major laws regulating the use and disclosure of PII.74.
12. Describe the data management concerns regarding the collection of data to support insurance operations.

For each assignment, define or describe each of the Key Terms and Concepts and answer each of the Review and Discussion Questions.

Key Terms and Concepts

Accident-Year Method of Aggregation:

Accounting information:

Actuary:

Allocated Loss Adjustment Expense:

Calendar-Year Method of Aggregation:

Casualty Actuary:

Claim:

Class rating:

Combined Ratio:

Construction class:

Dynamic Data:

Earned Premium:

Expense Ratio:

Hit ratio:

Incurred Losses:

Indemnity Payments:

Initial Reserve or Case Reserve:

Inspection reports:

Insurance scores:

Long-Tailed Lines:

Loss Adjustment Expense:

Loss Development:

Loss Ratio:

Medical examination:

Mix of business:

National Association of Insurance Commissioners (NAIC):

Persistent Data:

Personally Identifiable Information (PII):

Policy period:

Policy-Year Method of Aggregation:

Premium Audit:

Public Protection Classification:

Rating Variables:

Reserves:

Scopes Manual:

Statistical agents:

Unallocated Loss Adjustment Expense:

Underwriting:

Underwriting Expenses:

Underwriting Loss:

Underwriting Profit:

Unearned Premium:

Unearned Premium Reserve:

Written Premium:

Review Questions

1) Describe the types of information collected by insurers to support their operations.

2) Identify sources of information that insurers use.

3) Describe why insurers use external information.

4) Describe the considerations involved in using different sources of information.

5) Define the rating variable and give examples for different lines of insurance.

6) Describe how insurance companies use premium and loss information to monitor their operations.

7) Describe different methods of aggregating premium and loss data.

8) Define the concepts of dynamic data and persistent data.

9) Define Personally Identifiable Information (PII) and describe the rationale for the regulation of its use and disclosure.

10) What are some of the major laws regulating the use and disclosure of PII?

11) Describe the data management concerns regarding the collection of data to support insurance operations.

Discussion Questions

NOTE: The questions below are intended to continue to challenge you to test your knowledge of the required reading by applying what you have studied to real-life situations.

No suggested answers are provided at the end of the assignment for these types of open discussion questions. Answers may vary by student and will depend on their organization's culture, resources, and processes.

1) Give a real-life example of dynamic and persistent data.

2) How does your company handle aggregation of data for the various lines of insurance?

3) Discuss some of the methods you or your colleagues have used to make a decision or come to a conclusion when ensuring compliance with laws in data management.

4) For one day, observe and record all the external areas where data is sent.

Answers to Assignment 2 Questions

NOTE: These answers are provided to give students a basic understanding of acceptable types of responses. They are often not the only valid answers and are not intended to provide an exhaustive response to the questions.

Key Terms and Concepts

Accident-Year Method of Aggregation: In the accident-year method, earned premiums are also calculated from accounting records in the same way as they are in the calendar-year method. The difference between the calendar-year method and the accident-year method lies in how incurred losses are calculated. The accident-year method includes only those accidents or other events that gave rise to a claim that occurred during the specified twelve-month period, regardless of when they were reported or settled.

Accounting information: The function in insurance companies that provides information about the organization's value to owners, investors, and creditors; performance information to managers; solvency information to regulators; and tax obligations to tax authorities.

Actuary: A professional skilled in the analysis, evaluation, and management of the financial implications of future contingent events primarily with respect to general insurance, including property, casualty, and similar risk exposures.

Allocated Loss Adjustment Expense: Expenses that can be directly linked to a particular claim, for example, lawyers' fees in a liability claim or fees paid to an appraiser for assessing vehicle damage after a collision loss, are referred to as allocated loss adjustment expenses (ALAE).

Calendar-Year Method of Aggregation: The calendar-year method aggregates all premiums earned and all losses incurred during a single calendar year, regardless of when the associated policies were issued, or when the incidents giving rise to the claims actually occurred.

Casualty Actuary: A professional skilled in the analysis, evaluation, and management of the financial implications of future contingent events primarily with respect to general insurance, including property, casualty, and similar risk exposures.

Claim: A request that the insurer pay defined amounts of money when a covered loss occurs.

Class rating: A variable rating system in which applicants and loss exposures are classified based on selected characteristics.

Combined Ratio: The sum of the loss and expense ratios. It is a measure of an insurer's operating profit or loss, without factoring in any investment income.

Construction class: A classification system developed by the Insurance Services Office (ISO) to categorize buildings based on their resistance to fire damage.

Dynamic Data: Data that is current, active, and changing. In the context of insurance, dynamic data includes transactional data, policy data for current policies, HR information for current employees, claims information for open claims, and current sales information.

Earned Premium: At a given point in the policy term, the written premium for which the insurer has already provided coverage is referred to as earned premium.

Expense Ratio: An insurer's expense ratio is an indication of the organization's ability to control expenses and the costs it incurs to write and service business. It is calculated by dividing the insurer's incurred underwriting expenses by its written premiums.

Hit ratio: The percentage of quotations provided to potential customers that result in an actual sale.

Incurred Losses: An insurer's incurred losses are the sum of the indemnity payments made for that period, the allocated loss adjustment expenses incurred for that period and the reserves for outstanding claims at the end of the period.

Indemnity Payments: The claim settlement payments insurers make to insureds and claimants.

Initial Reserve or Case Reserve: When a claim is submitted to an insurer, in most cases the loss adjuster or claims system is required to quickly estimate the value of the loss and set aside that amount of funds allocated to that claim.

Inspection reports: Inspection reports describe such things as the construction, physical condition, and maintenance of the premises; the applicant's business operations; any risk control measures the applicant has implemented; and the organization's workplace safety record. These reports can also provide an evaluation of the organization's management.

Insurance scores: Insurance scores are developed to provide underwriting insights by examining credit reports, financial statements, and other tools for insureds or potential insureds, for use in jurisdictions where the practice is allowed.

Long-Tailed Lines: Certain lines of business are more prone to having claims remain open for extended periods. These lines of insurance are often called long-tail lines.

Loss Adjustment Expense: The sum of ALAE and ULAE is simply referred to as loss adjustment expenses (LAE).

Loss Development: The process through which loss data matures from the estimates used as reserves to the known ultimate settlement value of claims.

Loss Ratio: An insurer's loss ratio measures the success of its underwriting policies and practices. The loss ratio is calculated by dividing incurred losses by earned premiums.

Medical examination: An examination, typically conducted by life insurers on insured or potential insured, to measure the insurance applicant's height, weight, and blood pressure, obtain blood and urine samples, and may require the performance of other tests.

Mix of business: The distribution of different types of policies or insureds within an overall book of business.

National Association of Insurance Commissioners (NAIC): An association comprising insurance regulators from the 50 states, the District of Columbia, and the four U.S. territories to provide a forum for the development of uniform standards and policies where uniformity is appropriate.

Persistent Data: Persistent data, sometimes referred to as static data, is data that an insurer maintains and may use infrequently, for example, for analysis or reporting, but the data do not change. Examples of persistent data include policy data for canceled policies or claims data for settled claims that are not expected to be reopened.

Personally Identifiable Information (PII): Any information that can be used to uniquely identify, contact, or locate an individual, either alone or in conjunction with other sources, such as their name, Social Security number, driver's license number, date of birth, place of birth, mother's maiden name, and genetic information.

Policy period: The duration of the policy. Policy period may be a year, but it can be shorter or longer.

Policy-Year Method of Aggregation: In the policy-year method, data are aggregated for all premium and loss transactions associated with a particular group of policies written during a specified twelve-month period called the policy year.

Premium Audit: At the end of the policy term, the insurer conducts a premium audit to determine whether the actual sales revenues or payroll costs for the period were greater or less than projected.

Public Protection Classification: ISO also evaluates communities' public fire protection services and assigns each community a Public Protection Classification based on the extent and quality of those services.

Rating Variables: The characteristics an insurer uses to classify applicants and loss exposures are referred to as rating variables; the rates used vary based on those characteristics.

Reserves: The loss amounts for outstanding claims at the end of the period. The period-end reserves reflect any increases and decreases to reserves during the period.

Scopes Manual: The National Council on Compensation Insurance (NCCI) publishes the Scopes Manual, which is a tool underwriters can use to correctly classify applicants for workers' compensation coverage.

Statistical agents: State insurance departments designated agents to collect specific data.

Statistical plans: Statistical agents develop statistical plans that define the specific data insurers are to provide, the way in which insurers are to code and submit the data, and when they are to be submitted.

Unallocated Loss Adjustment Expense: Expenses that cannot be directly related to a particular claim; for example, claims adjusters' salaries are unallocated loss adjustment expenses (ULAE).

Underwriting: Underwriting is the process of evaluating the relative risk of loss that insurance applicants represent, assessing their acceptability, determining the appropriate coverage to provide, correctly classifying risks, selecting the appropriate rate based on their classification, and calculating premiums based on those rates.

Underwriting Expenses: Underwriting expenses include commissions paid to agents and brokers, advertising and other expenses incurred to acquire business, certain general expenses associated with the insurer's operations, taxes, licenses, and fees.

Underwriting Loss: When expressed as a percentage, a combined ratio above 100% indicates an underwriting loss.

Underwriting Profit: When expressed as a percentage, a combined ratio of less than 100% indicates that the insurer has posted an operating profit, usually referred to as an underwriting profit.

Unearned Premium: The difference between the written premium and the earned premium is referred to as unearned premium.

Unearned Premium Reserve: Insurers are required to create unearned premium reserves within their accounting records from which returned premiums can be paid.

Written Premium: The amount of premium for the policy, whether it is paid at inception or in installments. That amount is entered into the insurer's accounting records, but it is not considered to be revenue at that point.

Review Questions

1) Describe the types of information collected by insurers to support their operations.

Insurers collect information about an insured or potential insured's health, financials, and specific property information (such as a home, an automobile, or other property that may be the subject of insurance). Insurers are typically interested in information about people, things, or loss exposures to be insured.

2) Identify sources of information that insurers use.

Insurers collect information from some or all of the following sources: applications, producers, prior carriers, inspections, medical examinations, guides and tools, government records, credit reports, financial statements, accounting records, internal underwriting and claims information, technological devices, internet and social media, and claims analytics.

3) Describe why insurers use external information.

An insurer uses external information to analyze and understand the risks it assumes, as not all the information it needs can be found internally.

4) Describe the considerations involved in using different sources of information.

When analyzing different sources of information, one must consider issues related to quality, detail, timeliness, currency, and cost.

5) Define the rating variable and give examples for different lines of insurance.

The rating variable is the classification of applicants and loss exposures based on their characteristics. Examples of rating variables are driver age, gender, vehicle model year, and accident history for personal automobile insurance.

6) Describe how insurance companies use premium and loss information to monitor their operations.

Insurance companies typically use premium and loss information from the loss ratio, expense ratio, and combined ratio. The loss ratio, calculated by dividing incurred losses by earned premiums, measures the effectiveness of their underwriting policies and practices. The expense ratio, which measures the ability to control expenses and costs, and the combined ratio, the sum of the loss and expense ratios, help businesses indicate whether they posted an operating profit or loss.

7) Describe different methods of aggregating premium and loss data.

Premium and loss data are generally aggregated using the calendar-year method, the accident-year method, and the policy-year method. The calendar-year method aggregates all premiums earned and all losses incurred during a single calendar year. In the accident-year method, earned premiums are only those accidents or other events that gave rise to a claim that occurred during the specified twelve-month period, regardless of when they were reported or settled. In the policy-year method, data are aggregated for all premium and loss transactions associated with a particular group of policies written during a specified twelve-month period called the policy year, regardless of when the losses occur, or are reported, reserved, and settled.

8) Define the concepts of dynamic data and persistent data.

Dynamic data are data that are current, active, and changing, such as transactional data, policy data for current policies, HR information about current employees, claims information on open claims, or current sales information. Persistent data, sometimes referred to as static data or data that does not change, such as past policy or claims data.

9) Define Personally Identifiable Information (PII) and describe the rationale for the regulation of its use and disclosure.

Personally identifiable information (PII) is defined as any information that can be used to uniquely identify, contact, or locate an individual, either alone or in conjunction with other sources, such as their name, Social Security number, driver's license number, date of birth, place of birth, mother's maiden name, and genetic information. PII is subject to numerous laws and regulations at international, federal, and state levels regarding its collection, use, handling, and disposal, mainly to protect consumers' personal information and balance insurers' need for information with the public's need for fairness and privacy.

10) What are some of the major laws regulating the use and disclosure of PII?

The following regulations provide direction about the use and disclosure of PII:

- The Financial Services Modernization Act (Gramm-Leach-Bliley Act).
- Health Insurance Portability and Accountability Act (HIPAA).
- Consumer Privacy Protection Act.
- NAIC Insurance Information and Privacy Protection Model Act.

11) Describe the data management concerns regarding the collection of data to support insurance operations.

Insurance operations depend on data analysis and management, making data collection a necessary activity. The industry is highly regulated, and managers work to ensure the data they collect is of high quality and integrity, and that they comply with data security, privacy, and reporting requirements.

A Foundation for Data Solution Design

Educational Objectives

Upon completion of this assignment, you should be able to:

1. Define strategic, tactical, and operational management.
2. Identify the information needs of different levels of management and measures of key insurance company activities.
3. Define management reporting and describe common management reporting goals.
4. Describe how scorecards and dashboards facilitate management reporting.
5. Identify the types of information that might be found in a management dashboard and describe how the different managers might use it.
6. Explain why it is important to select and use metrics carefully.
7. Define responsibility accounting and explain how it facilitates management reporting.
8. Describe the data management concerns for management reporting.

For each assignment, define or describe each of the Key Terms and Concepts and answer each of the Review and Discussion Questions.

Key Terms and Concepts

Dashboard:

Management reporting:

Operational management:

Responsibility accounting:

Scorecard:

Strategic management:

Subrogation:

Tactical management:

Review Questions

1) Describe the types of information collected by insurers to support their operations.

2) Define strategic, tactical, and operational management.

3) Identify the information needs of different levels of management and measures of key insurance company activities.

4) Define management reporting and describe common management reporting goals.

5) Describe how scorecards and dashboards facilitate management reporting.

6) Identify the types of information that might be found in a management dashboard and describe how the different managers might use it.

7) Explain why it is important to select and use metrics carefully.

8) Define responsibility accounting and explain how it facilitates management reporting.

9) Describe the data management concerns for management reporting.

Discussion Questions

NOTE: The questions below are intended to continue to challenge you to test your knowledge of the required reading by applying what you have studied to real-life situations.

No suggested answers are provided at the end of the assignment for these types of open discussion questions. Answers may vary by student and will depend on their organization's culture, resources, and processes.

1) Give a real-life example of strategic, tactical, and operational management experience.

2) How does your company handle scorecards and reporting? What are the challenges and what are the causes of the challenges, both internal and external?

3) Discuss some of the methods by which decisions are made or come to a conclusion in your organization when the various levels of management decisions are working efficiently.

4) Observe and record all the information in the various dashboards and how management uses it.

Answers to Assignment 3 Questions

NOTE: These answers are provided to give students a basic understanding of acceptable types of responses. They are often not the only valid answers and are not intended to provide an exhaustive response to the questions.

Key Terms and Concepts

Dashboard: A business intelligence application that consolidates, aggregates, and graphically presents performance metrics against goals, enabling managers to monitor information at a glance.

Management reporting: The process that provides an organization's decision-makers with the information required for planning, managing, and measuring progress toward objectives at all three management levels.

Operational management: The process of organizing, leading, and controlling, at the frontline level, the resources and activities necessary for the successful implementation of tactical plans and the day-to-day delivery of the organization's products and services.

Responsibility accounting: An accounting approach that enables organizations to monitor and evaluate the performance of each individually managed area within the organization, from the frontline to senior management.

Scorecard: A "business intelligence application that helps manage an organization's performance by reporting a standard set of performance measurements against objectives, internal targets, and industry benchmarks.

Strategic management: The process of organizing, leading, and controlling, at an enterprise-wide level, the resources required to ensure that the organization achieves its strategic objectives.

Subrogation: When claim payments are made to insureds, an insurer is often able to recoup some, or even all, of those amounts from other sources.

Tactical management: The process of organizing, leading, and controlling projects and activities at the departmental or regional level.

Review Questions

1) Describe the types of information collected by insurers to support their operations.

The information needs of managers can vary significantly depending on their level, role, and function.

2) Define strategic, tactical, and operational management.

Strategic management is the process of organizing, leading, and controlling at an enterprise-wide level by senior management for a long-term view of the organization. Tactical management is the process by which middle managers organize, lead, and implement projects and activities that senior managers have put in place at the departmental or regional level. Operational management is the process of organizing and leading the implementation of tactical plans and the routine products and services of the organization.

3) Identify the information needs of different levels of management and measures of key insurance company activities.

Senior management needs information about the organization as a whole across various time periods for comparison and contrast to support strategic management of the business. Since middle management is concerned with tactical management, their information needs are more detailed, current, and frequent, possibly to meet regulatory requirements or to support the strategic direction set by senior managers. Operational managers need information to ensure routine deliverables of the organization are being met and provide reports to higher levels of managers of the firm.

4) Define management reporting and describe common management reporting goals.

Management reporting supports the management's information requirements for measuring performance and planning for all levels of operations. Management reports help the company achieve its goals of accuracy, timeliness, conciseness, focus, readability, clarity, flexibility, and exchangeability.

5) Describe how scorecards and dashboards facilitate management reporting.

In addition to traditional paper reports, information required by management is delivered through scorecards and dashboards. Scorecards and dashboards are similar in that they are business intelligence applications that consolidate, aggregate, and graphically present performance measurements relative to goals. While scorecards are used strategically, dashboards are used for tactical and operational purposes. Scorecards provide information for a chosen period, while dashboards provide information in real time.

6) **Identify the types of information that might be found in a management dashboard and describe how the different managers might use it.**

The type of information in a management dashboard depends on the objectives, structure, and culture, as well as the function the information supports. While high quality and dependability are desired in all reports, the level of granularity and detail in management dashboards must also support management's requirements. Underwriting managers' dashboards include information such as the number of policies in force and the mix of business. Information for claims managers' dashboards may include the number of claims, status, duration or cycle time, and other costs associated with claims, such as employees taken to serve, referrals to SIUs, etc. Finance managers are concerned with financial performance; hence, their dashboards contain financial data such as premiums, cash flow, net income, investment earnings, investment mix, return on equity, economic value added, and the number of days it takes accounting staff to release financial statements. Correspondingly, sales, service, marketing, and other departments need relevant information in their dashboards to run analytics and monitor trends.

7) **Explain why it is important to select and use metrics carefully.**

When choosing the metrics for the dashboards, it is important to select those that support the organization's objectives. Metrics should also be chosen to support interdepartmental collaboration and forward-thinking evaluation, furthering the company's vision and goals.

8) **Define responsibility accounting and explain how it facilitates management reporting.**

Responsibility accounting is an accounting approach that enables organizations to monitor and evaluate the performance of each individually managed area, from the frontline to senior management. The insurer's accounting records would need to be organized so that appropriate revenue and expense information can be tracked at the unit, group, and department levels, and later aggregated to generate results by division or the organization as a whole. Responsibility accounting involves preparing a budget, monitoring performance, providing performance reports, and making adjustments as necessary.

9) **Describe the data management concerns for management reporting.**

Since management reporting provides important information at all levels, data managers must ensure reports are high-quality, have integrity and security, allow integration, and include appropriate metadata.

.

Data Management and the Underwriting Function

Educational Objectives

Upon completion of this assignment, you should be able to:

1. Define and explain some basic underwriting terms and concepts.
2. Explain the difference between line and staff underwriting functions and describe their information needs.
3. Describe the process of underwriting a policy.
4. Describe how underwriting varies for different lines of insurance.
5. Describe the kinds of data that underwriters use, explain how they use them, and describe the considerations involved in the data collection process.
6. Explain how content and document management help underwriters.
7. Explain how property and casualty data managers support and add value to underwriters.

For each assignment, define or describe each of the Key Terms and Concepts and answer each of the Review and Discussion Questions.

Key Terms and Concepts

Beneficiaries:

Binder:

Ceding:

Ceding commission:

Coinsurance provision:

Excess reinsurance:

Exposure unit:

Facultative reinsurance:

Hazard:

Individual rating:

Insurable interest:

Insured:

Judgment rating:

Legal hazard:

Life insured:

Line underwriters:

Manuscripting:

Moral hazard:

Morale hazard or attitudinal hazard:

Per-claim excess:

Per-event excess:

Physical hazard:

Policyholder or Policy owner:

Primary insurer:

Pure risk:

Quota share reinsurance:

Reinsurance premium:

Reinsurance:

Reinsurer:

Retention or attachment point (reinsurance):

Retrocessionaires:

Risk:

Staff underwriters:

Speculative risk:

Treaty reinsurance:

Review Questions

1) Define and explain some basic underwriting terms and concepts.

2) Explain the difference between line and staff underwriting functions and describe their information needs.

3) Describe the process of underwriting a policy.

4) Describe how underwriting varies for different lines of insurance.

5) Describe the kinds of data that underwriters use, explain how they use them, and describe the considerations involved in the data collection process.

6) Explain how content and document management help underwriters.

7) Explain how property and casualty data managers support and add value to underwriters.

Discussion Questions

NOTE: The questions below are intended to continue to challenge you to test your knowledge of the required reading by applying what you have studied to real-life situations.

No suggested answers are provided at the end of the assignment for these types of open discussion questions. Answers may vary by student and will depend on their organization's culture, resources, and processes.

1) Give a real-life example of how effective data management helped underwriting, and how the lack of it caused a problem.

2) How does your company handle document management and content management?

3) Discuss some of the methods you or your colleagues have used to make a decision or come to a conclusion when deciding the type of data an underwriter receives and the criteria given importance for the decision.

4) In this assignment, we discussed how information such as the COPE model and public protection class is important for property insurance. Determine one line of insurance relevant to your work, and for one day, observe and record all the types of information relevant to the underwriting of that line of insurance.

Answers to Assignment 4 Questions

NOTE: These answers are provided to give students a basic understanding of acceptable types of responses. They are often not the only valid answers and are not intended to provide an exhaustive response to the questions.

Key Terms and Concepts

Beneficiaries: The people, or organizations, that policy owners select to receive the proceeds of life insurance policies.

Binder: A temporary agreement that an insured can use as proof of coverage until the formal policy is issued.

Ceding: The process by which a primary insurer transfers a portion of its financial liability for the loss exposure it writes to another insurer (typically called the reinsurer).

Ceding commission: The amount paid by the reinsurer to the primary insurer for incurring the cost of writing the business that is being ceded to the reinsurer.

Coinsurance provision: The percentage of covered losses or expenses that the insured is required to pay before the insurer becomes responsible to pay.

Excess reinsurance: In excess reinsurance, a primary insurer pays all losses up to its retention amount, and the reinsurer pays the excess above that amount up to the reinsurance policy's limit.

Exposure unit: The unit of measure (e.g., area, gross receipts, payroll) used to determine an insurance policy premium.

Facultative reinsurance: A reinsurance agreement negotiated and purchased for individual loss exposures.

Hazard: A situation or characteristic that would increase the applicant's chance of suffering a covered loss or increase the severity of any covered loss that might occur.

Individual rating: When risks are rated based on their individual characteristics, it is called individual rating.

Insurable interest: An entity has an insurable interest in a thing or a person if that entity faces a financial loss if the thing is damaged or destroyed, or the person is injured or dies.

Insured: The person or organization covered by the policy.

Judgment rating: When underwriters determine the rate based on the insurer's underwriting guidelines, knowledge of the risk, and the underwriter's own judgment and experience.

Legal hazard: A legal hazard can arise from the legal environment in a particular jurisdiction.

Life insured: The person covered by the policy in life insurance.

Line underwriters: The front-line staff responsible for day-to-day underwriting functions. They implement the underwriting guidelines and pricing structures developed by the staff underwriters.

Manuscripting: The process by which underwriters manually change the policy language for particularly large or complex accounts when the standard forms or a collection of forms are insufficient.

Moral hazard: A situation or condition that could induce an insured to lower the caution exercised, commit fraud by intentionally causing a loss, or exaggerate the value of a legitimate loss that occurs.

Morale hazard or attitudinal hazard: An attitude of carelessness or indifference that can develop in some people after they purchase insurance.

Per-claim excess: A type of excess reinsurance covering the amount of a single claim that exceeds the primary insurer's retention, up to the excess reinsurance policy's limit.

Per-event excess: A type of excess reinsurance where the reinsurer pays the excess above the primary insurer's retention for a single catastrophe, such as a hurricane, up to the reinsurance policy's limit.

Physical hazard: A physical condition that increases the likelihood or severity of a loss.

Policyholder or Policy owner: One or more organizations, persons, or entities whose name appears on the policy.

Primary insurer: The company that assumes the risk from the policyholder or policy owner. In a reinsurance arrangement, the primary insurer is the ceding insurer.

Pure risk: The category of risk where there is a chance of loss but no chance of gain.

Quota share reinsurance: When the reinsurer assumes a percentage of the risk on ceded policies, it is known as quota share reinsurance.

Reinsurance premium: The insurance premium that the primary insurer pays the reinsurer for the financial protection provided under the reinsurance agreement.

Reinsurance: The transfer of a portion of risk from one insurance company to another.

Reinsurer: An insurance organization that assumes a portion of the risk a primary insurer assumes when writing business.

Retention or attachment point (reinsurance): The underlying amount of risk retained by the primary insurer is the retention; the attachment point is the amount beyond which the reinsurer pays all losses. The attachment point refers to the specified amount of loss above which a reinsurer will pay up to the reinsurance policy's limit. Retention is the specified amount of loss the primary insurer is responsible for paying before the reinsurer begins to pay.

Retrocessionaires: Reinsurance organizations that assume risk from other reinsurers.

Risk: Risk is generally used to refer to one of two concepts:

- The possibility of financial loss; and
- The subject of insurance is either an application or a policy.

Staff underwriters: Staff underwriters are generally experienced, knowledgeable, senior underwriting staff who set underwriting policy and develop underwriting guidelines.

Speculative risk: The category of risk in which there is a chance of loss but also a chance of gain.

Treaty reinsurance: A reinsurance agreement (or treaty) between the primary insurer and the reinsurer that applies to all policies or loss exposures covered by the treaty.

Review Questions

1) Define and explain some basic underwriting terms and concepts.

Some basic terms and concepts in underwriting relate to risk, the uncertainty about the future, also the subject of insurance; matching risks and rates, which is the activity of setting rates insurers are allowed to charge based on underwriting and applicable statutes, rules, and regulations; and reinsurance, the transference and sharing of the financial consequences of certain specified types of loss.

2) Explain the difference between line and staff underwriting functions and describe their information needs.

Staff underwriters are generally in the insurer's head office or regional office to set underwriting policy and develop underwriting guidelines, develop new products and pricing structures, make rate adjustments, negotiate reinsurance, and perform underwriting audits. Line underwriters participate in day-to-day risk selection; implement staff underwriters' underwriting guidelines, direct producers; and manage the profitability of a specific book of business. Provide service to assigned producers; if licensed, may serve insureds directly. Staff underwriters manage line underwriters, and sometimes the producer serves as the line underwriter.

As for information needs, staff underwriters require premium and loss data, information from insurer advisory organizations, claims analytics, predictive modeling, third-party vendors, and the external environment, whereas line underwriters need information about applicants, the subjects of insurance, and loss exposures by line and territory.

3) Describe the process of underwriting a policy.

The underwriting process involves reviewing an insurance application, considering the hazards and exposures, making decisions about acceptance or adjustment, and issuing appropriate paperwork.

4) Describe how underwriting varies for different lines of insurance.

Differences in underwriting based on line of insurance depend on whether it is a one-time activity or a repetitive process, the level of automation, and the volume of information needed.

5) Describe the kinds of data that underwriters use, explain how they use them, and describe the considerations involved in the data collection process.

Underwriters' information needs depend on the unit of exposure, as the acceptance/rejection of the risk and premium determination are based on it. Their information needs vary due to the differences in the rating basis for each line of insurance. Physical damage exposures, liability loss exposures, life and health exposures, and workers' compensation exposures all differ; underwriting factors can vary widely by line of business.

6) Explain how content and document management help underwriters.

Content management enables distinct content elements to be stored, published, used, and reused in a variety of ways. Effective document and content management enables underwriters to discover, identify, and access the specific information they need to make informed decisions. Document management allows an underwriter to discover, find, and access a risk control report completed on an applicant's facility in the past.

7) Explain how property and casualty data managers support and add value to underwriters.

Data management professionals support underwriters by:

a.   enhancing data quality,
b.   ensuring data security,
c.   maintaining data integrity,
d.   increasing data integration,

e. improve access to high-quality information,

f. ensuring that the data collected is useful, and

g. creating clear data definitions and structuring data to facilitate "what if" analysis.

Performing the data management function well enables more effective underwriting policies and guidelines, better pricing schemes, and more innovative products and services. Data managers' ability to facilitate better underwriting decisions at both the staff and line levels can lead to enhanced underwriting profitability for the insurer.

Data Management and the Underwriting Function

Educational Objectives

Upon completion of this assignment, you should be able to:

1. Define and explain the basic claims terms and concepts.
2. Explain the life cycle of a claim.
3. Describe the types of external data a claims adjuster might use.
4. Describe how claims are adjusted.
5. Describe how the process of adjusting claims might vary for different lines of insurance.
6. Identify functional responsibilities within the claims department.
7. Describe the information needs of the claims department.
8. Identify and describe the internal reporting needs of the claims department.
9. Identify uses of claims data and information.
10. Describe how content and document management help claims personnel.
11. Explain the roles and responsibilities of the insurance data management function with respect to the claims function.

For each assignment, define or describe each of the Key Terms and Concepts and answer each of the Review and Discussion Questions.

Key Terms and Concepts

Accident date:

Additional living expenses:

Appraisal provision:

Arbitration:

Average value method:

Claimant:

Claims-made policy:

Claims-made trigger:

Claims adjusters:

Claims adjusting:

Claim examination:

Claim examiners:

Coinsurance clause:

Comparative negligence:

Compensatory damages:

Contributory negligence:

Damages:

Estoppel:

Exclusion:

Expert system method:

Exposure year:

Extended reporting period:

Face amount or face value:

Field adjuster:

Final report:

Formula method:

General damages:

Indemnify:

Independent adjusting firm:

Individual case method:

Inside adjusters:

Investigative report:

Mediation:

Mini-trial:

Multiple perils policies:

Named perils policies:

Negligence:

Nonwaiver agreement:

Notice date:

Occurrence policies:

Occurrence trigger:

Peril:

Preexisting condition:

Preliminary report:

Proof of loss:

Punitive damages:

Report date:

Report year:

Reservation of rights letter:

Retroactive date:

Roundtable method:

Scheduled injuries:

Special damages:

Spoliation of evidence:

Status report:

Waiver:

Review Questions

1) Define and explain some basic claims terms and concepts.

2) Explain the life cycle of a claim.

3) Describe the types of external data a claims adjuster might use.

4) Describe how claims are adjusted.

5) Describe how the process of adjusting claims might vary for different lines of insurance.

6) Identify functional responsibilities within the claims department.

7) Describe the information needs of the claims department.

8) Identify and describe the internal reporting needs of the claims department.

9) Identify uses of claims data and information.

10) Describe how content management helps claims personnel.

11) Describe how document management helps claims personnel.

12) Explain the roles and responsibilities of the insurance data management function with respect to the claims function.

Answers to Assignment 5 Questions

NOTE: These answers are provided to give students a basic understanding of acceptable types of responses. They are often not the only valid answers and are not intended to provide an exhaustive response to the questions.

Key Terms and Concepts

Accident date: The date of the occurrence of a covered peril that led to the claim is referred to as the accident date.

Additional living expenses: Additional living expenses cover costs the insured incurs if the home is not fit to occupy during repairs, such as hotel accommodation.

Appraisal provision: A policy provision outlining a specific process for resolving disagreements over the value of a claim.

Arbitration: The process in which a third party, the arbitrator, considers each party's position to determine the outcome of the case.

Average value method: The average value method in settling or reserving a claim uses analysis of previously settled claims, by type, to determine the average value paid for each particular type of claim.

Claimant: The person claiming compensation from the insurance company is referred to as the claimant.

Claims-made policy: A claims-made policy covers claims reported during the policy period.

Claims-made trigger: The occurrence of a covered peril reported during the policy period of a claims-made policy.

Claims adjusters: Claims adjusters or claim representatives are the individuals responsible for investigating, determining coverage, and settling claims.

Claims adjusting: The process of settling or otherwise investigating claims, determining whether losses are covered, establishing the value of losses, and paying claimants the settlements to which they are entitled.

Claim examination: In life and health insurance, the process for handling claims is called claim examination.

Claims examiners: In life and health insurance, the employees responsible for investigating claims, determining whether losses are covered, establishing the value of losses, and paying claimants the settlements to which they are entitled are called claim examiners, claim approvers, claim analysts, or claim specialists.

Coinsurance clause: A coinsurance clause reduces the amount of a claim settlement proportionally if the damaged building is underinsured.

Comparative negligence: An insurance principle where the insured defendant and the plaintiff third party share the financial consequences of a loss in proportion to their respective levels of fault.

Compensatory damages: Compensatory damages are paid by an insurer to compensate a third party for the harm they have suffered due to the insured's negligence.

Contributory negligence: An insurance principle under which injured parties are barred from recovering damages if their own negligence contributed to the harm they suffered.

Damages: The financial loss to the insured due to payments to a third party.

Estoppel: The legal principle that prohibits a party from asserting a claim or right that is inconsistent with that party's past statement or conduct on which another party has detrimentally relied.

Exclusion: Exclusion is wording in a policy that specifically disallows coverage for a type of property, a set of circumstances, or a cause of loss.

Expert system method: The expert system method of case reserving relies on software that applies pre-established rules to the circumstances of individual claims and sets reserves based on these conditions and the insurer's historical experience with similar claims.

Exposure year: The year in which a claim has a trigger, such as the accident or notice date.

Extended reporting period: The extended reporting period is the additional time allowed for reporting claims under a claims-made policy.

Face amount or face value: The face amount or face value is the fair settlement value of a life insurance policy, which is the death benefit on the policy.

Field adjuster: Field adjusters work outside the office, inspecting loss scenes, investigating losses, and meeting with insureds, claimants, and attorneys.

Final report: Final reports describe the conclusion of a claim, including the basis of settlement or the reason(s), for denial.

Formula method: The formula method establishes a mathematical formula based on statistical analysis to calculate case reserves or settlements for different types of claims.

General damages: General damages are payments made by the insurer intended to compensate for such things as "pain and suffering" and "emotional suffering."

Indemnify: To indemnify means to restore insured and claimants to the same financial position they were in before a covered loss occurred.

Independent adjusting firm: An independent adjusting firm handles an insurer's claims for a fee.

Individual case method: The individual case method is a method for settling or adjusting a case reserve, in which adjusters use their judgment to estimate the ultimate value of a claim based on previous experience with similar claims.

Inside adjusters: Inside adjusters handle claims without leaving the insurer's office.

Investigative report: A full, formal claims report that describes the information already obtained, outlines any additional information that needs to be developed, and provides an evaluation of coverage, liability, and potential damages.

Mediation: A process in which a knowledgeable third party, such as a retired judge, listens to each party's arguments, evaluates each party's position, and works with the parties to help them reach a mutually acceptable settlement.

Mini-trial: In cases of dispute in the claims process, a mini-trial is a method of arriving at a mutually acceptable agreement between the parties by presenting their arguments to a knowledgeable individual or panel, who provides an opinion on the likely outcome if the case were to go to court.

Multiple perils policies: These policies provide coverage for any cause of loss not specifically excluded in the policy wording.

Named perils policies: The specific perils named for the causes of loss for which the insurance policy allows or disallows coverage.

Negligence: The failure to exercise the degree of care that a reasonable person in a similar situation would exercise to avoid harming others.

Nonwaiver agreement: A signed agreement indicating that during the course of the investigation, neither the insurer nor the insured waives rights under the policy.

Notice date: The date the insured notifies the insurer of the occurrence of an incident that may lead to a claim.

Occurrence policies: Policies that respond to losses that occur within the policy period.

Occurrence trigger: The occurrence of a covered peril that led to the claim is referred to as the trigger.

Peril: The causes of loss for which the insurance policy allows or disallows coverage

Preexisting condition: A condition that began before the policy's original inception date.

Preliminary report: An adjuster must file a preliminary report within a specified period to provide an initial evaluation of any potential coverage issues or liability considerations that need to be investigated.

Proof of loss: A sworn statement of the facts associated with a claim, including the date and cause of loss, an inventory of the property damaged or destroyed, the amount of the loss, and details of any other insurance that might apply.

Punitive damages: Additional damages awarded with the intention of punishing a wrongdoer.

Report date: The date that the insurance company receives the claim is the report date.

Report year: Report year data is data from claims reported in a particular year.

Reservation of rights letter: A letter sent by the adjuster to the insured indicating that the insurer does not waive its rights under the policy.

Retroactive date: The date after which coverage begins for the insured's liability coverage with the insurer.

Roundtable method: A method of settling or reserving a claim based on several adjusters' independent reviews and their agreement on an appropriate amount.

Scheduled injuries: The predetermined method for calculating claim payments for various injuries.

Special damages: Special damages are paid by an insurer to reimburse actual expenses or losses a third party has incurred.

Spoliation of evidence: Failure to preserve evidence is referred to as spoliation of evidence. The insured's or insurer's inability to preserve the evidence may hamper the ability to prove the cause due to which the injury occurred.

Status report: Periodic reports filed by claims adjusters to keep supervisors and managers informed of the status and progress of claims and to facilitate the adjustment of case reserves.

Waiver: The intentional relinquishment of a known right.

Review Questions

1) **Define and explain some basic claims terms and concepts.**

Some basic terms and concepts in claims include insurance policy coverage, limits, losses, indemnification, exclusions, and coverage triggers. They also include claims adjusting, adjusters, matching risks and rates (the activity of determining the amounts insurers are allowed to pay), applicable statutes, rules, and regulations; and reinsurance, the transfer and sharing of the financial consequences of certain specified types of loss.

2) **Explain the life cycle of a claim.**

Claims departments may be in the insurer's head office or regional office, or claims may be managed by independent adjusting firms appointed by the insurer. The claims department may first receive a notice of loss or a claim; this information is acknowledged and given to a claims adjuster. If necessary (or standard procedure exists), a special adjuster may verify and/or investigate all facts about the claim. Claims adjusters evaluate the information provided by the claimant to determine coverage based on definitions, terms and conditions and exclusions. If a claim is not covered, a denial is sent; if it is covered, then a case reserve is determined. The adjuster may request proof of loss before determining the amount and/or number of indemnifications, and settling and closing the claim.

3) Describe the types of external data a claims adjuster might use.

The claims process involves reviewing the claim, considering the hazards and exposures, making decisions about acceptance or adjustment, ascertaining deductibles, and issuing accurate, organized paperwork. They may use information from external data sources such as specialist (or field) adjusters, professional appraisers, witnesses, technological devices, the internet and social media, subject matter experts such as accountants or governmental agencies. Claims professionals may also use information available in legislation, the litigation process, fraud detection and prevention, and changes and trends that affect claim settlement.

4) Describe how claims are adjusted.

Claims are adjusted based on the provisions of the policy regarding the extent of coverage, limits, and exclusions; proofs provided by the claimant; applicable rules and regulations; possible appraisers' reports; and, finally, negotiations with the claimant to settle the claim.

5) Describe how the process of adjusting claims might vary for different lines of insurance.

Claims adjusting is different for the various lines of insurance due to the variety of considerations in indemnifying the claimant in accordance with the provisions of the insurance policy. Property insurance policies take into account the value of the loss and the cost of additional expenses as they pertain to the property value covered by the policy. Liability claims can arise from a variety of wrongs. Bodily injury policies may consider medical expenses and costs incurred for medical treatment, and thus depend on an opinion from medical experts. Life insurance, on the other hand, is adjusted to the loss of life by a covered event.

6) Identify functional responsibilities within the claims department.

In the claims management discipline, claims adjusters or representatives handle claims in the company's offices, while field adjusters may visit the subject insured to inspect, appraise, and meet with other subject-matter experts, such as attorneys. A senior claims executive establishes claims policies and procedures, sets reserves, determines reinsurer involvement, and oversees audits. Claim examiners perform the basic claims function in life insurance companies, claim approvers, claim analysts, or claim specialists. Some attorneys in the claims department advise based on legislation and defend insurers in suits from insureds, claimants, and others. Some insurers have employees in the claims department responsible for salvage, subrogation, special investigations, reinsurance recoveries, and related activities.

7) Describe the information needs of the claims department.

As for information needs, claim data are available for use in analysis and pricing. Senior executives use the data for planning and policy setting, as well as for audits. Some data may be in the form of preliminary, status, investigative, regulatory, or final reports. For better planning and projections, executives require premium and loss data; information from insurer advisory organizations, claims analytics, predictive modeling, third-party vendors, and the external environment; information about applicants and the subjects of insurance; and intelligence about loss exposures by line and territory.

Data management professionals support underwriters by:

- enhancing data quality,
- ensuring data security,
- maintaining data integrity,
- increasing data integration,
- improve access to high-quality information,
- ensuring that the data collected is useful, and
- creating clear data definitions and structuring data to facilitate "what if" analysis.

Performing the data management function well enables more efficient claims policies and guidelines, better claims reserving and settlement practices, and more innovative products and services. Data managers' ability to facilitate better claims decisions can result in cost control for the insurer.

8) Identify and describe the internal reporting needs of the claims department.

The claims department needs documentation and data to be organized for some or all of the following internal uses:

- record keeping,
- investigations,
- financial planning for payment schedules,
- prepare for compliance and legal proceedings,
- analysis and evaluation of efficiency and improvements in processing,
- develop metrics for predictions about the cause of losses, reserves,
- understand timelines of the various events in the policy and claim life cycle,
- be defensible to internal customers, insureds, and external stakeholders.

9) Identify uses of claims data and information.

Claims data and information are used in some or all of the following ways by insurers:

- actuarial inputs for loss cost calculations of individual policies,
- calculation of costs by various metrics such as the cause of loss, demographics,
- comparative loss analysis to identify claimants with a higher propensity to file claims,
- comparative analysis by line of insurance or timelines of claims events,
- comparative analysis with relation to industry data,
- identifying new product offerings to serve customers, optimizing exposure control,
- identifying gaps in underwriting or premium calculations,

- fraud detection,
- managing the reinsurance process.

10) Describe how content management helps claims personnel.

Content management helps claims personnel stay organized by enabling them to recall any transaction detail and make changes as necessary for financial and process efficiency. This helps with proper strategic planning, better rapport with all stakeholders, and a reputation for competence, capable of performing or functioning in the best possible manner with the least waste of time and effort, having and using requisite knowledge, skill, and expertise.

11) Describe how document management helps claims personnel.

Document management helps personnel stay organized by allowing them to recall any transaction detail and make changes as necessary for financial and process efficiency.

12) Explain the roles and responsibilities of the insurance data management function with respect to the claims function.

Data management can help evaluate the efficiency of each stage and each member of the claims cycle. The claims department needs data about the insured, the claimant, or the facts of the claim. Analysis of data on the policy under which the claim is being made, along with the timelines, also helps senior managers develop and revise policies for the claims management process.

Actuarial Pricing of Property and Casualty Products

Educational Objectives

Upon completion of this assignment, you should be able to:

1. Define and explain basic actuarial terms and concepts.
2. Outline some of the principles and standards that property and casualty actuaries follow.
3. Explain why premium data need to be adjusted for use in ratemaking.
4. Explain why loss data needs to be adjusted for use in ratemaking.
5. Explain the importance of matching premium and loss experience for ratemaking.
6. Explain why different methods of aggregating premium and loss experience are used for ratemaking.
7. Describe what an actuary considers when making an actuarial judgment.
8. Describe the similarities and differences between ratemaking for workers' compensation and other property and casualty lines of insurance.
9. Describe the growing use of predictive modeling for actuarial analyses.
10. Explain the roles and responsibilities of the insurance data management function with respect to the actuarial function.

For each assignment, define or describe each of the Key Terms and Concepts and answer each of the Review and Discussion Questions.

Key Terms and Concepts

Actuarial Standards Board (ASB):

Administered pricing system or rating bureau:

Advisory rate system:

Balance sheet:

Base rate:

Casualty Actuarial Society (CAS):

Catastrophes:

Contingencies loading:

Discounting:

Earned exposures:

Exposure base:

Experience period:

Experience rating modification:

Exposure unit:

Extension of exposures:

Fixed expense:

In-force exposures:

In-force premiums or premiums in force:

Judgment method:

Loss cost system:

Loss ratio method:

Multivariate method:

Opportunity cost:

Parallelogram method:

Pure premium:

Policyholders' surplus:

Ratemaking:

Rating engine:

Rate relativity factors:

Rating plan:

Residual market mechanisms:

Return on equity:

Risk-free interest rate:

Shareholders' equity or owners' equity:

Shock losses:

Ultimate loss:

Unearned exposures:

Valuation date:

Variable expense:

Written exposures:

Review Questions

1) What is an actuary?

2) What is ratemaking?

3) What is a rating plan?

4) What is an exposure unit? Define exposure base and provide examples of the exposure base used for a few lines of business/coverage.

5) Define written exposures and provide an example.

6) Define earned exposures and provide an example.

7) Define unearned exposures and provide an example.

8) Define in-force exposures and provide an example.

9) Define in-force premiums.

10) Explain the time value of money and provide an example of this concept.

11) What is discounting?

12) What purpose do future and present value calculations serve in general and in insurance?

13) Describe the concept of opportunity cost.

14) What is a balance sheet?

15) Define shareholders' equity.

16) What is the goal of ratemaking?

17) Briefly describe the ratemaking process.

18) List the ratemaking approaches used by insurers to adjust historical loss and premium data.

19) Explain how the loss ratio method works.

20) Explain how the pure premium method works.

21) The loss ratio and pure premium methods require access to past loss and premium data. What would an insurer do if there is no past experience?

22) What is a challenge associated with the judgment method?

23) In the judgment method, what would be considered relevant external data?

24) What are rate relativity factors and what do they ensure?

25) Besides the three traditional approaches to ratemaking, what other methods have developed?

26) What is an advantage of using the multivariate methods for ratemaking?

27) Name two organizations in the United States that promote actuarial principles and standards.

28) How does the CAS promote actuarial principles and standards?

29) Describe a few examples of Statements of Principles published by the CAS.

30) How does the ASB promote actuarial principles and standards?

31) Describe a few examples of the Actuarial Standards of Practice published by the ASB.

32) List some of the Actuarial Standards of Practice published by the ASB that are relevant to property and casualty ratemaking.

33) What is "on-leveling"?

34) What are some factors that need to be considered when adjusting historical premium data?

35) Describe the purpose of a premium audit.

36) What are the two commonly used methods for adjusting historical premium data?

37) Describe the parallelogram method.

38) Describe the extension of exposures.

39) What are the advantages and disadvantages of the parallelogram method?

40) What are the advantages and disadvantages of the extension of the exposure method?

41) Why is it necessary to adjust historical loss data from the experience period?

42) What trends and changes do actuaries need to consider when adjusting historical loss data?

43) What is loss development and why is it necessary?

44) What does an actuary's estimated ultimate loss consist of?

45) Why is IBNR and IBNER included in the ultimate loss estimates?

46) Why is the selection of a valuation date for losses important?

47) Why are shock and catastrophe losses treated separately from historical loss data?

48) What are some ways that an actuary would handle shock and catastrophe losses?

49) Why is it necessary that the losses and premiums being aggregated are matched appropriately?

50) What are the methods by which premium and loss data are aggregated for use in ratemaking?

51) Describe the calendar-year data aggregation method.

52) What are the advantages/disadvantages of the calendar-year data aggregation method?

53) How is the accident-year method different/similar to the calendar-year method?

54) Identify an advantage of the accident-year method over the calendar-year method.

55) Describe the policy-year method.

56) What are the advantages/disadvantages of the policy-year data aggregation method?

57) When exercising actuarial judgment, what are some of the factors considered by actuaries?

58) What should be considered in selecting an exposure unit?

59) What should be considered in defining classification plans and individual risk rating?

60) What should be considered in identifying the data to use and how the data is organized?

61) What should be considered regarding the homogeneity and credibility of the data?

62) Define credibility.

63) What should be considered during loss development and the handling of shock and catastrophe losses?

64) What should be considered when evaluating policy provisions, the mix of business and operational changes?

65) What should be considered when reviewing reinsurance, recovery vehicles, and investment income?

66) What are rates based on in workers' compensation insurance?

67) What is the exposure unit for most workers' compensation insurance?

68) What is unique about workers' compensation compared to other lines of business?

69) What are the three types of systems under which workers' compensation ratemaking organizations operate?

70) Describe the three types of systems under which workers' compensation ratemaking organizations operate.

71) Of the three types of systems under which workers' compensation ratemaking organizations operate, which one applies to most of the states?

72) How is workers' compensation ratemaking similar to other property and casualty lines?

73) How is workers' compensation ratemaking different from other property and casualty lines?

74) What are the five broad industry categories in workers' compensation insurance?

75) What is the definition of analytics as used by IDMA?

76) What are the three disciplines into which analytics is divided?

77) How are descriptive, predictive, and prescriptive analytics used?

78) Describe predictive modeling.

79) What is a hallmark of the predictive modeling approach?

80) What are some benefits of having access to an increasing volume and variety of data at a granular level?

81) In what areas do data managers provide value to the actuarial function?

82) How does the data manager provide value to the area of data quality?

83) How does the data manager's role provide enhanced decision making to the actuarial function?

84) How does the data manager provide value to the area of internal data coordination?

85) How does the data manager provide value to the area of compliance?

Answers to Assignment 6 Questions

NOTE: These answers are provided to give students a basic understanding of acceptable types of responses. They are often not the only valid answers and are not intended to provide an exhaustive response to the questions.

Key Terms and Concepts

Actuarial Standards Board (ASB): The Actuarial Standards Board (ASB) "establishes and improves standards of actuarial practice."

Administered pricing system or rating bureau: An administered pricing system is one in which the ratemaking organization, typically called a rating bureau, develops rates for use by all insurers offering workers' compensation insurance coverage within a state.

Advisory rate system: In an advisory rate system, the ratemaking organization develops advisory rates only. The insurers have the option to adopt the rates either as advised or with modifications.

Balance sheet: Lists the organization's assets and liabilities.

Base rate: The base rate for a particular line of business is the rate the insurer must charge per exposure unit to cover losses and expenses and earn a reasonable profit.

Casualty Actuarial Society (CAS): The Casualty Actuarial Society (CAS) works to advance property and casualty actuarial science through research and education.

Catastrophes: Events that cause $25 million or more in direct insured losses to property and affect a significant number of policyholders and insurers.

Contingencies loading: The additional amount added to the base rate, intended to provide a financial buffer in the event that actual losses exceed projections.

Discounting: The process of determining the present value of a payment or a stream of payments that is to be received in the future.

Earned exposures: An insurer's earned exposure is the portion of the premium for which the coverage period has already passed (therefore, the premium is already earned).

Exposure base: The way exposure units are defined. Exposure bases can vary by line of business and by coverage. For example, in automobile insurance, the exposure base traditionally used is one vehicle insured for one year, or one car-year. For workers' compensation coverage, payroll is the usual exposure base.

Experience period: A specified historical period during which loss and premium data are collected for use in ratemaking. The experience period can vary by line of business or by coverage.

Experience rating modification: An experience rating or experience rating modification adjusts a policyholder's premium up or down based on their loss experience relative to that of other policyholders in the same classification.

Exposure unit: The unit of measure (for example, area, gross receipts, payroll) used to determine an insurance policy premium.

Extension of exposures: A sophisticated method of adjusting historical premium data that involves rerating each policy for each year of the experience period using current rates. This method requires the development and use of a rating engine.

Fixed expense: Fixed expenses include all non-loss-adjusting expenses (non-LAE) that do not change with price.

In-force exposures: The exposure units for which the insurer may be required to pay losses.

In-force premiums or premiums in force: The total written premiums associated with in-force exposures at any point in time are referred to as in-force premiums or premiums in force.

Judgment method: A ratemaking method in which the actuary determines rates based on experience and actuarial judgment.

Loss cost system: In a loss cost system, the rates developed by the rating organization reflect only anticipated future losses and loss adjustment expenses. Each insurer using a rating organization's loss costs must factor in its own anticipated expenses, as well as profit and contingencies, to develop its own rates.

Loss ratio method: A ratemaking method used to modify existing rates. It indicates the required percentage change (either increase or decrease).

Multivariate method: Multivariate ratemaking methods are sophisticated techniques used by actuaries in ratemaking to better identify interrelationships and correlations among rating variables, resulting in more refined and accurate rate relativities.

Opportunity cost: The benefit a person could have received but gave up to take another course of action. It reflects the fact that if funds or other resources are invested in one manner, they are unavailable for other profitable uses.

Parallelogram method: The parallelogram method (also known as the geometric method) is a method for adjusting historical premium data. It involves modifying the data for each year during the experience period by a factor to bring those premium data to an approximation of current rate levels.

Pure premium: The amount required to pay losses and LAE, and it is calculated by dividing the value of incurred losses by the number of earned exposure units.

Policyholders' surplus: On an insurer's balance sheet, shareholders' equity is referred to as policyholders' surplus.

Ratemaking: The process of establishing rates for insurance or other risk transfer mechanisms.

Rating engine: A collection of components that allows an insurer's systems to calculate accurate premiums based on a wide variety of underwriting parameters and rules.

Rate relativity factors: Rate relativity factors, or rating factors, are the factors by which actuaries adjust the base rate for other risk classes. These factors ensure that the overall rate level change is not affected by the distribution of that change across the different rating classifications.

Rating plan: A method for classifying risks and calculating premiums based on a selected group of rating variables, exposure units, and rates.

Residual market mechanisms: Residual market mechanisms provide insurance coverage that cannot be obtained from insurers operating in the voluntary insurance market.

Return on equity: Measures an insurer's profit as a proportion of its shareholders' equity, the money invested by its shareholders. It shows how well or how poorly investors have fared over a given period.

Risk-free interest rate: The rate of return investors would receive on investments with a relatively risk-free investment, such as T-bills, would be referred to as the risk-free interest rate.

Shareholders' equity or owners' equity: The resulting profit or loss when liabilities are subtracted from assets.

Shock losses: Large losses that may significantly increase an insurer's incurred losses.

Ultimate loss: The amount of money required to settle all claims associated with a selected group of policies is referred to as the ultimate loss.

Unearned exposures: The portion of the exposure for which coverage is ongoing or in the future is considered the unearned exposure. In other words, it is the difference between the insurer's written exposures and earned exposures.

Valuation date: The cutoff date for adjustments made to paid claims and reserve estimates in a loss report.

Variable expense: Expense that varies proportionally with the premium charged, for example, premium taxes and producers' sales commissions.

Written exposures: The number of exposures underwritten having inception dates within a specified period, such as a calendar year.

Review Questions

1) **What is an actuary?**

An actuary is a professional skilled in the analysis, evaluation, and management of the financial implications of future contingent events, primarily with respect to general insurance, including property, casualty, and similar risk exposures.

2) What is ratemaking?

Ratemaking is the process of establishing rates used in insurance or other risk transfer mechanisms. The process results in the production of a rating plan. Ratemaking can involve developing rates for new products or adjusting rates for existing products.

3) What is a rating plan?

A rating plan is a method for classifying risks and calculating premiums based on a selected group of rating variables, exposure units, and rates.

4) What is an exposure unit?

An exposure unit is "the unit of measure (for example, area, gross receipts, payroll) used to determine an insurance policy premium". It is a measure of the amount of loss exposure the insurer is assuming.

5) Define exposure base and provide examples of the exposure base used for a few lines of business/coverage.

An exposure base is the way in which exposure units are defined. Exposure bases can vary by line of business and by coverage. For example, for personal automobile coverage, the exposure base used is one vehicle insured for one year (or one car-year). Another example of an exposure base used is payroll for workers' compensation coverage. For product liability insurance, gross sales are typically used as the exposure base.

6) Define written exposures and provide an example.

Written exposures are the number of exposures an insurer has underwritten with inception dates within a specified time period, such as a calendar year. For example, an automobile insurer writes four annual policies, one at the beginning of each quarter over the course of a calendar year, covering one vehicle per policy. In this example, the insurer's written exposures are four since the annual policies covered four automobiles with inception dates falling within the relevant calendar year.

7) Define earned exposures and provide an example.

Earned exposures are the portion of the exposure for which the coverage period has already passed. For example, an automobile insurer writes four annual policies, one at the beginning of each quarter over the course of a calendar year, covering one vehicle per policy. In this example, the insurer's earned exposures is 2.5 since it has earned (i) a full car-year for the policy starting January 1st, (ii) three-quarters of a car-year for the policy starting April 1ˢᵗ, (iii) half a car-year for the policy starting July 1ˢᵗ and (iv) a quarter car-year for the policy starting October 1ˢᵗ.

8) Define unearned exposures and provide an example.

Unearned exposures are the difference between the insurer's written exposures and earned exposures. For example, an automobile insurer writes four annual policies, one at the beginning of each quarter over the course of a calendar year, covering one vehicle per policy. In this example, the insurer's unearned exposure is 1.5 (the written exposure of 4 minus the earned exposure of 2.5).

9) Define in-force exposures and provide an example.

In-force exposures are the exposure units for which an insurer may be required to pay a loss. For example, an automobile insurer writes four annual policies, one at the beginning of each quarter over the course of a calendar year, covering one vehicle per policy. In this example, on June 10ᵗʰ, the insurer would have two in-force exposures (the cars insured under the policies with inception dates of January 1ˢᵗ and April 1ˢᵗ.

10) Define in-force premiums.

In-force premiums are the total written premiums associated with in-force exposures at any point in time. In-force premiums are also known as premiums in force.

11) Explain the time value of money and provide an example of this concept.

The basic concept of the time value of money is that a dollar today is generally worth more than a dollar received at some point in the future because the dollar in hand today can be invested to earn interest.

Let's take an individual with $100 invested over five years, earning 5% interest per year. At the end of the five-year period, the investor would have $127.64, assuming the individual leaves both the interest and the principal invested throughout the entire five-year period. In this example, the promise of $100 five years from now is worth $27.64 less than $100 in hand today.

12) What is discounting?

Discounting is the process of determining the present value of a payment or a stream of payments to be received in the future. It is a process for determining how much money an individual would need to invest today at a given rate of compound interest to have a specified amount in the future.

13) What purpose do future and present value calculations serve in general and in insurance?

In general, these calculations are often used to compare the relative attractiveness of different types of projects or investments. In insurance, present value calculations can be used in reserving to determine how much money needs to be set aside now to meet future obligations to policyholders and claimants. Future value calculations can be used on the types of claims that take a relatively long time to settle to discount the future value of long-tail claims.

14) Describe the concept of opportunity cost.

The concept of opportunity cost reflects the fact that if funds or other resources are invested in one way, they are unavailable for other profitable uses.

15) What is a balance sheet?

A balance sheet is a financial statement that lists an organization's assets and liabilities.

16) Define shareholders' equity.

Shareholders' equity is the assets minus the liabilities on an organization's balance sheet. It is also referred to as owners' equity. On an insurer's balance sheet, shareholders' equity is referred to as policyholders' surplus.

17) What is the goal of ratemaking?

The goal of ratemaking is to ensure that the premiums an insurer charges for policies written during a future period are sufficient to cover anticipated losses, loss adjustment expenses, and underwriting expenses, as well as to generate a reasonable underwriting profit.

18) Briefly describe the ratemaking process.

Ratemaking begins with the collection of loss and premium data from a specified historical period called the experience period. The experience period varies by line of business and by coverage, depending on the stability of the line of business. Data is aggregated using the calendar-year, accident-year, or policy-year method. Within a particular line of business, loss exposures are classified based on selected rating variables. Each class is rated differently from others based on its relative degree of risk. Insurers select one of these classes as the base risk to which the base rate applies. Finally, adjustments are made to the historical loss and premium data collected using various ratemaking approaches.

19) List the ratemaking approaches used by insurers to adjust historical loss and premium data.

The ratemaking approaches are the (a) loss ratio method, (b) pure premium method, (c) judgment method, and (d) multivariate method.

20) Explain how the loss ratio method works.

The loss ratio method is used to modify existing rates. It indicates the required percentage change (either increase or decrease). This method starts by identifying the target loss ratio by subtracting a percentage for variable expenses and underwriting profit from 100 percent. The indicated rate change is calculated as the sum of the projected loss and LAE ratio, and the fixed expense ratio divided by the target loss ratio less 100 percent. A positive result indicates a rate increase is necessary, whereas a negative result indicates a rate decrease is required.

21) Explain how the pure premium method works.

The pure premium method is used to modify existing rates by developing an indicated average rate. Similar to the loss ratio method, the insurer first identifies the target loss ratio. The indicated average rate is calculated as the sum of the pure premium and fixed underwriting expense per exposure divided by the target loss ratio. A positive result means a rate increase is needed, whereas a negative result indicates a rate decrease is in order.

22) The loss ratio and pure premium methods require access to past loss and premium data. What would an insurer do if there is no past experience?

When there is no past experience, actuaries would use the judgment method. The actuary determines rates based on their experience and actuarial judgment. The process involves gathering as much relevant external data as possible, if available.

23) What is a challenge associated with the judgment method?

A challenge associated with the judgment method is obtaining relevant external data.

24) In the judgment method, what would be considered relevant external data?

For external data to be considered relevant, it must be derived from business that is similar in kind and quality to the new business the insurer proposes to write. If insurance-specific data (such as that provided by a data collection organization) cannot be obtained, the data may need to be assembled and integrated from different sources, for example, our court systems or labor department statistics.

25) What are rate relativity factors and what do they ensure?

Rate relativity factors (or rating factors) are the factors by which actuaries adjust the base rate for other risk classes.

They ensure that the overall rate level change is not affected by the distribution of that change across different rating classifications. In other words, if rates in a particular state increase by 6%, the individual risk classifications may experience a rate change that is either more or less than 6%, depending on their contribution to the overall loss experience.

26) Besides the three traditional approaches to ratemaking, what other methods have been developed?

As computing power has increased and insurers have developed data warehouses and populated them with increasingly granular data, actuaries have been able to apply more sophisticated multivariate methods.

27) What is an advantage of using the multivariate methods for ratemaking?

These methods allow actuaries to better identify interrelationships and correlations among rating variables, resulting in more refined and accurate rate relativities.

28) Name two organizations in the United States that promote actuarial principles and standards.

The Casualty Actuarial Society (CAS) and the Actuarial Standards Board (ASB).

29) How does the CAS promote actuarial principles and standards?

The CAS publishes Statements of Principles intended to provide broad guidance in the development of actuarial procedures and standards of practice. Each brief Statement includes an introduction clarifying the scope of the document, definitions of terms used, guiding principles, a discussion of associated considerations (where applicable), and a conclusion.

30) Describe a few examples of Statements of Principles published by the CAS.

One example is the CAS Statement of Principles Regarding Property and Casualty Insurance Ratemaking. It includes four principles that support the objective that rates should be reasonable, not excessive, not inadequate, and not unfairly discriminatory.

Another example is the CAS Statement of Principles Regarding Property and Casualty Valuations. It focuses on the process of determining, at a point in time, the financial condition of an insurer or other property and casualty risk bearer, such as a reinsurer. It includes seven principles that provide guidance on the valuation of assets, obligations (e.g., losses and loss adjustment expenses), and considerations (e.g., premiums). It also includes a discussion on the data to be used in the valuation, the organization of that data, and its homogeneity and credibility.

31) How does the ASB promote actuarial principles and standards?

The ASB establishes and improves standards of actuarial practice. It publishes the Actuarial Standards of Practice (ASOP) that identify what an actuary should consider, document, and disclose when performing an actuarial assignment. ASOP includes a discussion of the scope and purpose of the document; a definitions section; an analysis of the issues related to the topic under review with recommended actuarial practices; and a section on communication and disclosures.

32) Describe a few examples of the Actuarial Standards of Practice published by the ASB.

One example is ASOP No. 12 Risk Classification (for All Practices). It provides guidance to actuaries when designing, reviewing, or changing risk classification systems. It discusses, among other things, the selection of characteristics that will form the basis of a risk classification system. It states that a risk characteristic should be directly related to expected outcomes. It should also be objective, practical, in compliance with applicable laws and consistent with industry practices and the organization's business practices.

Another example is ASOP No. 23 Data Quality. It provides guidance on selecting data, relying on data supplied by others, reviewing data, using data, and making disclosures about data quality.

33) List some of the Actuarial Standards of Practice published by the ASB that are relevant to property and casualty ratemaking.

- ASOP No. 13 Trending Procedures in Property/Casualty Insurance.
- ASOP No. 25 Credibility Procedures.
- ASOP No. 29 Expense Provisions in Property/Casualty Insurance Ratemaking.
- ASOP No. 38 Using Models Outside the Actuary's Area of Expertise (Property and Casualty).
- ASOP No. 39 Treatment of Catastrophe Losses in Property/Casualty Insurance Ratemaking.
- ASOP No. 40 Actuarial Communications.

34) What is "on-leveling"?

"On-leveling" is the adjusting of premiums from the experience period to current rate levels during the ratemaking process. This is necessary because rates have usually changed during the experience period.

35) What are some factors that need to be considered when adjusting historical premium data?

Some premiums from the most recent portion of the experience period may not yet be fully earned and may need to be projected to their fully earned value. Some recent premiums may be subject to adjustment, such as when the results of a premium audit have not yet been finalized. If an insurer's book of business is changing, the effect of those changes also needs to be considered. The premiums in some lines of business are affected by inflation and will increase even if the rate remains constant.

36) Describe the purpose of a premium audit.

Premium audits are needed for some lines of insurance that are rated based on factors such as sales revenue or payroll. At the beginning of the policy period, the insured organization's payroll costs or sales revenue are projections. The initial policy premiums are therefore estimated based on those projections. At the end of the policy period, the insurer conducts a premium audit to determine whether actual sales revenue or payroll costs were higher or lower than the projected amount. The premium audit will result in either an additional premium being charged to the insured or a refund of the premium to the insured.

37) What are the two commonly used methods for adjusting historical premium data?

The two methods are (a) the parallelogram method and (b) the extension of exposures.

38) Describe the parallelogram method.

The parallelogram method (or geometric method) involves modifying the data for each year during the experience period by a factor to bring the premium data to an approximation of current rate levels.

39) Describe the extension of exposures.

The extension of exposures method involves rerating every policy from each year of the experience period using current rates.

40) What are the advantages and disadvantages of the parallelogram method?

It is simple to implement but less accurate.

41) What are the advantages and disadvantages of the extension of exposures method?

It is more accurate but more difficult to implement. It requires the development of a rating engine. It can also be a challenge for data managers, as it may involve working with actuaries to make reasonable assumptions and inferences about rating attributes currently used but not collected during the experience period.

42) Why is it necessary to adjust historical loss data from the experience period?

It is necessary because losses need to be projected to determine the value of losses anticipated during the future period for which the new rates are being developed.

43) What trends and changes do actuaries need to consider when adjusting historical loss data?

The value of losses can change over time due to inflation or deflation. Social trends and changing attitudes can lead to modifications in laws and regulations that specify the types of losses an insurer must cover or the benefits that must be provided, potentially resulting in broader coverage. Court decisions regarding coverage or damages can set new precedents for future court actions, potentially increasing an insurer's future exposures. Any changes in insurer's participation in or subsidization of residual market mechanisms must also be considered. Over time, insurers may elect to amend the standard coverage offered, such as increasing a liability limit.

44) What is loss development and why is it necessary?

Loss development is the process through which loss data matures from the estimates used as reserves to the known ultimate settlement value of claims. The time it takes to settle a claim varies by insurance line. Some claims are reported and settled quickly. Others may be reported quickly but the ultimate settlement value will not be known for years. Others may still not be reported for years, and some claims take years to settle. Because claims allocated to the experience period may not be settled for many years, actuaries need to estimate loss development and project ultimate settlement values to ensure the loss data for long-tail claims are relatively accurate for use in ratemaking.

45) What does an actuary's estimated ultimate loss consist of?

An actuary's estimated ultimate loss includes (a) paid losses, (b) case reserves for those claims that have been reported but have not as yet been settled, (c) incurred but not reported reserves (IBNR) and (d) incurred but not enough reported reserve (IBNER).

46) Why are IBNR and IBNER included in the ultimate loss estimates?

It ensures that the loss data used in ratemaking is relatively accurate and that the proposed rates are adequate.

47) Why is the selection of a valuation date for losses important?

It allows for adjustments to the earliest years of the analysis period to reflect the most up-to-date estimate of the final value of claims.

48) Why are shock and catastrophe losses treated separately from historical loss data?

Because these losses are relatively rare, their inclusion in historical loss data could distort the data and lead to excessive rate increases. Additionally, these losses are typically subject to excess-of-loss reinsurance. During the ratemaking process, actuaries reduce loss projections to account for any excess-of-loss reinsurance recoveries.

49) What are some ways that an actuary would handle shock and catastrophe losses?

An actuary may cap these losses at a predetermined amount. In the case of shock losses, actuaries may require that claims paid at policy limits be flagged if the actual loss sustained by the insured or claimant exceeds that amount.

50) Why is it necessary that the losses and premiums being aggregated are matched appropriately?

Matching losses and premiums for a policy means that losses are matched with the premiums that generated the loss exposure. In this way, actuaries are better able to develop rates that will be adequate for the losses anticipated in the future.

51) What are the methods by which premium and loss data are aggregated for use in ratemaking?

The two typical aggregation methods are (a) accident-year and (b) policy-year. A third method is the calendar-year method, which is typically used in financial reporting or for ratemaking when claims for the coverage type are reported and settled relatively shortly after they occur.

52) Describe the calendar-year data aggregation method.

The calendar-year method aggregates earned premiums and incurred losses for a single calendar year, regardless of when the associated policies were issued or when the incidents giving rise to the claims actually occurred.

53) What are the advantages/disadvantages of the calendar-year data aggregation method?

The advantage is that the data becomes available reasonably quickly after year end and because they are compiled from accounting records they are inexpensive to obtain. The disadvantage is that this approach does not accurately match losses and premiums from the same policies.

54) How is the accident-year method different/similar to the calendar-year method?

Both calculate earned premiums from accounting records. However, the accident-year method includes only those accidents or other events that gave rise to a claim that occurred during the specified twelve-month period, regardless of when they were reported or settled. To avoid delays in compiling accident-year data, this method requires the insurer to estimate the value of losses that have occurred during the experience period but have not yet been reported, the value of changes in reserves, and any settlements that will be made after the end of the accident year.

55) Identify an advantage of the accident-year method over the calendar-year method.

The accident-year method matches premiums and losses more closely than the calendar-year method, since losses that occurred in the selected twelve-month period are compared with the premiums earned during that same period.

56) Describe the policy-year method.

In the policy-year method, data are aggregated for all premium and loss transactions associated with a particular group of policies written during a specified twelve-month period called the policy year. Policy-year incurred losses include claim settlements and case reserves for losses on policies written during the specified policy year, regardless of when the losses occurred, or when they are reported, reserved, or settled.

57) What are the advantages/disadvantages of the policy-year data aggregation method?

The policy-year method provides the best match of premiums and losses because it matches the premium earned for a particular policy with the claim or claims paid under that policy. The disadvantage is that at the end of the specified policy year, neither the amount of earned premiums nor the value of incurred losses is known. As a result, it takes time for policy-year premium and loss data to mature, which is the reason that policy-year data takes longer to compile than the other two data aggregation methods.

58) When exercising actuarial judgment, what are some of the factors considered by actuaries?

Actuaries consider a wide variety of factors when exercising judgment. These factors include (a) the exposure units used, (b) classification plans and individual risk rating, (c) the data that will be used and how the data is organized, (d) the homogeneity and credibility of the data, (e) loss development and handling of shock and catastrophe losses, (f) policy provisions, mix of business and operational changes and (g) reinsurance, other recovery vehicles and investment income.

59) What should be considered in selecting an exposure unit?

It should be selected to reflect the hazard associated with the coverage being provided, and it should be practical to use and readily verifiable.

60) What should be considered in defining classification plans and individual risk rating?

Risks need to be classified by their relative likelihood and probable loss severity to allow proper matching of risk and rate when pricing insurance products. When an individual risk's experience is sufficiently credible, the premium for that risk should be adjusted to reflect it. In these situations, consideration should be given to the impact of individual risk rating plans on an insurer's overall experience.

61) What should be considered in identifying the data to use and how the data is organized?

The data are relevant only to the extent that they provide a basis for developing a reasonable estimate of what is likely to happen in the future. It must be accurate, integrated, timely, and accessible for analysis. The data should be organized depending on the aggregation method to be used for the analysis.

62) What should be considered regarding the homogeneity and credibility of the data?

Subdividing groups into more homogeneous subsets helps increase the credibility of the information developed during analysis. However, a subset should still be large enough to be statistically credible.

63) Define credibility.

Credibility is a measure of the predictive value that an actuary attaches to a particular body of data.

64) What should be considered during loss development and the handling of shock and catastrophe losses?

Shock and catastrophe losses can distort historical loss data used in loss development. The inclusion of shock and catastrophe losses can lead to overestimated or underestimated projected losses. The actuary may need to remove these losses from the analysis. However, since these events do occur, the actuary needs to factor them back into the ratemaking analysis by including a catastrophe allowance in the rate.

65) What should be considered when evaluating policy provisions, the mix of business and operational changes?

If there have been changes to policy provisions, such as broadening or restricting coverage, increasing coverage limits, or modifying policy deductibles, the impact of those changes needs to be considered when projecting future loss values. The composition of an insurer's book of business may be changing, which can affect future loss severity and frequency and must be factored into the ratemaking process. Operational changes, such as case reserving, claims handling, or marketing practices, may affect the continuity of an insurer's loss and expense experience and, therefore, should be evaluated for their impact on ratemaking.

66) What should be considered when reviewing reinsurance, recovery vehicles, and investment income?

Insurers can recover a portion of the loss settlements they pay out from reinsurers through salvage and subrogation, as well as from other sources. Insurers may also generate investment income from the premiums they receive.

67) What are rates based on in workers' compensation insurance?

Workers' compensation rates are based on industry classification and job classifications.

68) What is the exposure unit for most workers' compensation insurance?

The exposure unit for most workers' compensation coverage is $100 of payroll per job classification.

69) What is unique about workers' compensation compared to other lines of business?

Workers' compensation is a unique line of business in that there are monopolistic states in which workers' compensation coverage can only be provided through the state's designated workers' compensation program, states with state-specific rating and statistical organizations, and a multistate statistical and rating organization.

70) What are the three types of systems under which workers' compensation ratemaking organizations operate?

The three types of systems are (a) administered pricing systems, (b) advisory rate systems, and (c) loss cost systems.

71) Describe the three types of systems under which workers' compensation ratemaking organizations operate.

Under an administered pricing system, the ratemaking organization (typically a rating bureau) develops rates for use by all insurers offering workers' compensation coverage in the state. The rates include components for anticipated future losses and expenses, as well as profit and contingencies. Under an advisory rate system, the ratemaking organization develops advisory rates only. The rates include components for anticipated future losses and expenses, as well as profit and contingencies. Each insurer may use the advisory rates or modify them. Under the loss cost system, the rates developed by the ratemaking organization reflect only anticipated future losses and loss adjustment expenses. Each insurer using these loss costs must factor in its own anticipated expenses, as well as profit and contingencies, to develop its own rates.

72) Of the three types of systems under which workers' compensation ratemaking organizations operate, which one applies to most of the states?

The loss cost system applies to the majority of states.

73) How is workers' compensation ratemaking similar to other property and casualty lines?

Historical loss and premium data from the experience period are adjusted to determine the amount of any required rate adjustment. Historical premium data are brought to current levels. Historical loss data are adjusted to reflect factors such as inflation, changes in medical treatments and costs, changes in workers' compensation benefits, changes in the workplace, and loss trends. Historical loss data are projected to a future period and compared with current rate levels to determine whether a rate increase or decrease is required, and the amount of change.

74) How is workers' compensation ratemaking different from other property and casualty lines?

The rating bureau calculates experience modification factors for individual employers. In other commercial lines of business, this is done by the insurance company. Workers' compensation coverage is required by the state, even if an employer wants to self-insure. Even with a large deductible, the mechanism is typically for the insurance company to pay the full loss and then recover the deductible from the employer. The nature of the coverage is state-mandated. For most lines of business, the insurance company is free to offer coverage of its choosing, often subject to approval. For workers' compensation insurance, there is almost no opportunity to do that.

The fundamental rating plan is highly uniform. Insurance companies rarely deviated from the definitions of workers' compensation job classes, even though they often devise their own class definitions for other lines of business. Because rating is based on job classes, it is largely one-dimensional, as opposed to personal auto, which uses a variety of rating variables, including age, gender, marital status, territory, type of vehicle, age of vehicle, and household composition.

Unlike workers' compensation, many lines of business (e.g., professional liability insurance) have little in the way of rating advisory services available.

75) What are the five broad industry categories in workers' compensation insurance?

The five broad industry categories in workers' compensation are (a) manufacturing, (b) contracting, (c) office and clerical, (d) goods and services, and (e) miscellaneous.

76) What is the definition of analytics as used by IDMA?

Analytics includes the data, tools, and applications that support corporate strategic plans and business performance; they enable the gathering, storage, access, and analysis of corporate data for decision-making.

77) What are the three disciplines into which analytics is divided?

Analytics is subdivided into (a) descriptive analytics, (b) predictive analytics, and (c) prescriptive analytics.

78) How are descriptive, predictive, and prescriptive analytics used?

Descriptive analytics presents a depiction of a past or current state. It provides the information used in predictive analytics, which focuses on determining what is likely to happen in the future based on historical trends and other data. Prescriptive analytics helps managers choose the best course of action when a decision needs to be made.

79) Describe predictive modeling.

Predictive modeling refers to data-mining technologies and tools used to create models that help predict future trends or outcomes.

80) What is a hallmark of the predictive modeling approach?

A hallmark of the predictive modeling approach is that the data need not be aggregated prior to analysis. The analysis can examine premiums, losses, and characteristics at the individual policy level. A key factor in this process is the ability to discover, access, and effectively manage an increasing volume and variety of data about individuals, organizations, and risks at a more granular level.

81) What are some benefits of having access to an increasing volume and variety of data at a granular level?

It allows an insurer to use internal and external data to better understand its policyholders and to more effectively evaluate the degree of potential risk each insured represents. An enhanced ability to manage data also allows the insurer to more closely analyze claims data and apply the results of that analysis in pricing its insurance products. For example, segmenting loss data by peril lets an insurer examine the benefit of offering a dead-bolt lock discount for the portion of the homeowner's premium that covers the theft peril. The discount would not be applied to the portion of the premium that covers the windstorm peril. Increased, integrated, well-managed, granular data enables insurers, advisory and rating organizations, financial services, healthcare providers, and other insurance-related organizations to optimize service levels and financial performance.

82) In what areas do data managers provide value to the actuarial function?

Data managers provide value to the actuarial function in four areas: (a) data quality, (b) enhanced decision-making, (c) internal data coordination and (d) ensuring regulatory compliance.

83) How does the data manager provide value to the area of data quality?

Good data management improves the validity, accuracy, reasonableness, completeness, and timeliness of the data on which actuaries rely, thereby enhancing their confidence in that data. When data quality is ensured, the actuary can focus on core professional responsibilities and actuarial decision making. Better-quality data also enhance the effectiveness of predictive modeling, allowing improvements to new and existing products and pricing.

84) How does the data manager's role provide enhanced decision making to the actuarial function?

Documented, controlled data management processes help ensure the validity of the data being used. This improves decision making and allows actuaries to explain and defend the decisions that have been made. Better actuarial decisions lead to better decisions, improved customer satisfaction and retention, and more customers.

85) How does the data manager provide value to the area of internal data coordination?

Effective data management allows for improved internal data coordination. This reduces the cost and time associated with data collection, storage, and dispersal, making data available more quickly. By promoting database interoperability and enabling better data integration, data managers provide actuaries with more options for using data. Data managers also advocate for implementing industry and enterprise data standards and for consistent data definitions and values. This helps ensure the quality of enterprise data and communication across its various sources.

86) How does the data manager provide value to the area of compliance?

Data management enhances compliance by ensuring the privacy and confidentiality of data and compliance with data reporting laws and regulations. Data managers assist in identifying solutions to data reporting issues and facilitating communications with regulators. They help ensure that regulatory perspectives are understood internally.

Property and Casualty Insurance Accounting

Educational Objectives

Upon completion of this assignment, you should be able to:

1. Define and explain basic actuarial terms and concepts.
2. Define and explain basic accounting terms and concepts.
3. Explain the origin of statutory accounting.
4. Discuss statutory accounting principles (SAP) and how they differ from generally accepted accounting principles (GAAP).
5. Compare and contrast financial and statistical data with respect to purpose and use.
6. Explain why the data manager needs to understand insurance accounting and reporting.
7. Identify the major components of an insurance company's Annual Statement.
8. Describe how loss adjustment expenses are treated in the Annual Statement.
9. Explain the roles and responsibilities of the insurance data management function with respect the accounting function.

For each assignment, define or describe each of the Key Terms and Concepts and answer each of the Review and Discussion Questions.

Key Terms and Concepts

Adjusting and other (A&O) expenses:

Admitted assets:

Amortization, or depreciation:

Asset:

Capital stock or owners' equity or retained earnings:

Cash flow statement or Statement of cash flow:

Conservatism:

Current asset:

Current liability:

Defense and cost containment (DCC) expenses:

Depreciation, or amortization:

Expenses:

Fixed asset:

Generally accepted accounting principles (GAAP):

Going-concern assumption:

Income statement or statement of income:

Intangible asset:

Jurat page:

Liability:

Liquidation assumption:

Long-term liabilities:

Matching principle:

Net investment income:

Non-admitted assets:

Policy acquisition costs:

Revenue:

Revenue recognition:

Sales commissions:

Statement of changes in owners' equity:

Statistical filings:

Statistical plans:

Statutory accounting principles (SAP):

Tangible asset:

Unit transaction coding:

Review Questions

1) Briefly describe accounting.

2) What are financial statements?

3) Provide some examples of financial statements.

4) What is a balance sheet?

5) Define and provide some examples of an asset.

6) How are assets classified?

7) Define and provide an example of a current asset.

8) Define and provide an example of a fixed asset.

9) Define and provide an example of a tangible asset.

10) Define and provide an example of an intangible asset.

11) Define liability for accounting purposes.

12) How are liabilities classified?

13) Define and provide an example of a current liability.

14) Define and provide an example of a long-term liability.

15) For entities other than insurers, what is the difference between total assets and liabilities on an organization's balance sheet?

16) For an insurer, what is another way to refer to owners' equity?

17) Describe GAAP and SAP.

18) How are SAP guidelines more conservative than GAAP?

19) Define and provide examples of admitted assets.

20) How does the balance sheet of an insurer differ from that of other organizations?

21) What is a statement of income (or income statement)?

22) What are other names for the income statement?

23) Briefly describe the information found on an insurer's statement of income.

24) What is the statement of cash flows?

25) What types of activities does the statement of cash flows focus on?

26) What is the statement of changes in owners' equity?

27) What are other names for the statement of changes in owners' equity?

28) What are the important considerations when compiling financial statements?

29) Define revenues and expenses.

30) Explain the GAAP principle of revenue recognition and how it is reflected in property and casualty insurance.

31) Explain the GAAP matching principle. Provide an example.

32) How does the matching principle work when an organization's assets have a useful life of many years? What is an example of such an asset?

33) Provide an example of how an asset would be depreciated.

34) What does the accounting principle of conservatism require when estimates are used?

35) What happens when an organization's expenses cannot be directly linked or matched to revenues? Provide an example of when this might occur.

36) How does the insurance industry differ from other industries?

37) Why do insurers have a greater risk of becoming insolvent than other organizations?

38) Provide some examples of how an insurer can become insolvent.

39) How did statutory accounting principles develop?

40) What are some of the fundamental differences between SAP and GAAP?

41) Briefly describe what assumptions are made in SAP and how it differs from GAAP.

42) Briefly describe how assets are treated in SAP and how they differ from GAAP.

43) Briefly describe how expenses are recognized in SAP and how it differs from GAAP.

44) What effect do the differences between SAP and GAAP have on the financial statements generated by an insurer?

45) Give examples of nonadmitted assets.

46) What are policy acquisition costs? Give examples.

47) What are the two types of data reporting regulations to which insurers are subject?

48) State the purpose served by each of the two types of data reported.

49) What is the source of financial and statistical data?

50) What is the Annual Statement?

51) How is the financial data in the Annual Statement reported?

52) How are statistical data reported to the regulators?

53) What is the difference between unit transaction coding and summary reporting in statistical data reporting?

54) Provide a few examples of unit transaction coding in statistical data reporting.

55) List a few differences between financial and statistical data.

56) Why is it important that data managers understand the differences between financial and statistical reporting, as well as the differences between SAP and GAAP?

57) What are the objectives of the data manager as they relate to insurance accounting?

58) How does the data manager achieve these objectives as it relates to insurance accounting?

59) What are the components of the NAIC Annual Statement?

60) Briefly describe the individual components of the NAIC Annual Statement.

61) List a few examples of the special schedules and supplements found in the NAIC Annual Statement.

62) In general, how does the NAIC treat loss adjustment expenses for reporting purposes?

63) When and how did the NAIC's treatment of loss adjustment expenses change for statutory financial reporting?

64) Define defense and cost containment (DCC) expenses. Provide some examples.

65) Define adjusting and other (A&O) expenses. Provide some examples.

66) What do data managers involved in the generation of these reports need to be aware of?

67) In what areas does effective data management add value?

68) How does the data manager add value in the statutory and financial accounting arena?

69) How does the data manager add value in the premium and loss transaction booking arena?

70) How does the data manager add value in the control of collections?

71) How does the data manager add value in the collection, storage, and dispersal of data?

72) How does the data manager add value in the strategic planning arena?

73) How does the data manager add value in the compliance arena?

Discussion Questions

NOTE: The questions below are intended to continue to challenge you to test your knowledge of the required reading by applying what you have studied to real-life situations.

No suggested answers are provided at the end of the assignment for these types of open discussion questions. Answers may vary by student and will depend on their organization's culture, resources, and processes.

1) Give a real-life example of how SAP is more conservative than GAAP.

2) How does your company handle the reporting of financial statements?

3) Discuss some of the methods you or your colleagues have used to make a decision or come to a conclusion when SAP reporting puts constraints on the company.

4) For one day, observe and record all the SAP reportable transactions.

Answers to Assignment 7 Questions

NOTE: These answers are provided to give students a basic understanding of acceptable types of responses. They are often not the only valid answers and are not intended to provide an exhaustive response to the questions.

Key Terms and Concepts

Adjusting and other (A&O) expenses: The remaining LAE that are not directly related to defense and cost containment, such as claims adjusters' salaries.

Admitted assets: Assets that can be easily turned into cash, such as bonds and stocks.

Amortization, or depreciation: The allocation of an item's cost over its useful life is referred to as depreciation or amortization.

Asset: A resource that an organization owns that can be used to produce economic benefit for that organization.

Capital stock or owners' equity or retained earnings: The difference between total assets and total liabilities represents the value—either positive or negative—of the organization to its owners. On an insurer's balance sheet, owners' equity is referred to as policyholders' surplus, or surplus as regards policyholders.

Cash flow statement or Statement of cash flow: The statement of cash flow is a financial statement that reconciles the amount of cash an organization has at the end of a period with the amount it had at the beginning of that same period by documenting the sources and uses of cash during the period.

Conservatism: The accounting principle of conservatism requires that, when estimations or approximations are used, financial statements should reflect the lowest reasonable net income for the period.

Current asset: A resource that can be used to produce economic benefit and/or one that can be converted to cash within twelve months.

Current liability: Liabilities that must be paid within twelve months are referred to as current liabilities.

Defense and cost containment (DCC) expenses: Expenses related to defending claims or managing the costs associated with claims.

Depreciation, or amortization: The allocation of an item's cost over its useful life is referred to as depreciation or amortization.

Expenses: Costs incurred to produce revenues; they decrease owners' equity.

Fixed asset: An asset that will not be converted into cash in the near future.

Generally accepted accounting principles (GAAP): Accounting guidelines and practices that focus on the measurement of an organization's earnings from period to period.

Going-concern assumption: Under GAAP, the underlying assumption is that an organization will continue in operation and generate revenues. This assumption is often referred to as the going-concern assumption.

Income statement or statement of income: The income statement or statement of income records the revenues received from sales and the costs involved in making those sales, as well as other expenses, such as taxes, and sources of profit, such as investments.

Intangible asset: A resource that can be used to produce economic benefit and has value but no physical substance; examples of intangible assets include copyrights, trade secrets, and data.

Jurat page: The first page of the NAIC Annual Statement. It provides general information about the insurance company, such as contact information and the names of its directors and officers.

Liability: Liabilities are debts or obligations that an organization owes to others that will require the relinquishment of economic assets or benefits.

Liquidation assumption: A liquidation assumption, or run-off assumption, is an accounting approach under GAAP. It applies when an organization is expected to terminate operations. This assumption only recognizes the sale or liquidation value of an organization's assets.

Long-term liabilities: Liabilities that do not need to be paid for a period beyond the current year.

Matching principle: Under the GAAP matching principle, when determining net income for a particular period, revenues are matched with the expenses that produced them.

Net investment income: Investment income minus investment losses and certain investment-related expenses.

Non-admitted assets: Under SAP, certain types of assets must be excluded from an insurer's balance sheet. These are called non-admitted assets and are usually either illiquid or statutorily disallowed.

Policy acquisition costs: Insurance carriers incur various expenses to underwrite insurance. These expenses are called policy acquisition costs and include sales commissions paid to agents and brokers, the cost of printing and mailing policies to policyholders, and state premium taxes.

Revenue: The funds organizations receive from the sale of products or the provision of services.

Revenue recognition: A GAAP principle that specifies that revenue is recognized at the time an exchange is made or a service is provided, rather than when payment is received.

Sales commissions: Remuneration paid to producers for placing policies with an insurer.

Statement of changes in owners' equity: A financial statement that shows any investments in the organization made by owners, including shareholders, and any disbursements made to them over a given period of time.

Statistical filings: Most regulators appoint statistical agents to collect data from insurers, compile it according to the formats specified by the regulator, and submit the compiled data to the regulator. These reports are referred to as statistical filings.

Statistical plans: Statistical plans provide specific instructions on the manner in which insurers must report premium and loss transactions to the statistical agent.

Statutory accounting principles (SAP): When compiling and submitting financial reports to insurance regulators, insurers must comply with an additional set of accounting rules and guidelines known as statutory accounting principles (SAP). These principles are more conservative than the generally accepted accounting principles.

Tangible asset: A tangible asset is something of value that has physical substance, such as a building, a vehicle, or a computer.

Unit transaction coding: When statistical reporting requires unit transaction coding, a statistical record is required for each policy transaction.

Review Questions

1) **Briefly describe accounting.**

Accounting is a process through which organizations collect, organize, interpret, record, and communicate information about their economic activities. It involves applying standards and principles, as well as exercising judgment in determining how they will be applied.

2) **What are financial statements?**

Financial statements are reports that document an organization's financial position at a particular point in time or its financial performance over a period of time.

3) **Provide some examples of financial statements.**

Some examples of financial statements are (a) balance sheet, (b) statement of income or income statement, (c) statement of cash flows, and (d) statement of changes in owners' equity.

4) **What is a balance sheet?**

A balance sheet is a financial statement that provides a snapshot of an organization's financial position at a given point in time, such as the end of a quarter or year-end. It lists an organization's assets and liabilities.

5) Define and provide some examples of an asset.

An asset is a resource that an organization owns that can be used to produce economic benefit for that organization at some time in the future. Examples of assets include cash, investments, inventory, buildings, patents, and accounts receivable.

6) How are assets classified?

Assets are classified into (a) current or fixed and (b) tangible or intangible.

7) Define and provide an example of a current asset.

A current asset is one that will be converted to cash within twelve months. For example, a manufacturer's present inventory would be considered a current asset.

8) Define and provide an example of a fixed asset.

A fixed asset is one that will not be converted into cash in the foreseeable future. An example of a fixed asset is a building in which an organization intends to remain housed indefinitely.

9) Define and provide an example of a tangible asset.

A tangible asset is something of value that has physical substance. Examples of tangible assets are a building, a vehicle, or a computer.

10) Define and provide an example of an intangible asset.

An intangible asset is one that has value but no physical substance. Examples of intangible assets are copyrights, trade secrets, and data.

11) Define liability for accounting purposes.

In accounting, liabilities are debts and obligations that an organization owes to others that will require the relinquishment of economic assets or benefits at some point in the future.

12) How are liabilities classified?

Liabilities are classified as current or long-term.

13) Define and provide an example of a current liability.

A current liability is one that must be paid within twelve months. An example would be payment for goods purchased on credit from a supplier.

14) Define and provide an example of a long-term liability.

A long-term liability is one that need not be paid until a future date. An example would be bonds.

15) For entities other than insurers, what is the difference between total assets and liabilities on an organization's balance sheet?

It represents the total value of the organization to its owners and is referred to as owners' equity or shareholders' equity. In some situations, it may also be called "capital".

16) For an insurer, what is another way to refer to owners' equity?

On an insurer's balance sheet, owners' equity is also referred to as policyholders' surplus or surplus as regards policyholders.

17) Describe GAAP and SAP.

Generally Accepted Accounting Principles (GAAP) are accounting guidelines and practices that focus on the measurement of an organization's earnings from period to period. GAAP is used to prepare financial statements for managers and third parties, such as investors and lenders, as well as the U.S. Securities and Exchange Commission (SEC) and the Internal Revenue Service (IRS). Statutory Accounting Principles (SAP) are additional accounting rules and guidelines that insurers must comply with when compiling and submitting financial reports to insurance regulators. They focus on whether a company has the ability to satisfy its obligations to policyholders and creditors at a given point in time.

18) How are SAP guidelines more conservative than GAAP?

Under SAP, insurers are restricted in the assets they can include on their balance sheets.

19) Define and provide examples of admitted assets.

Admitted assets are those that can be readily turned into cash and are therefore allowed to be included on an insurer's balance sheet under SAP. Examples of admitted assets are stocks and bonds.

20) How does the balance sheet of an insurer differ from that of other organizations?

A manufacturer's assets would include significant amounts for property, plant, and equipment. A retailer's assets would include a substantial investment in inventory. However, because insurers must be able to pay claims as they occur, their assets typically include a considerable volume of bonds, stocks, and other investments that can be sold quickly when the need for funds arises. An insurer's assets also include (a) premiums due from agents and brokers and (b) amounts that are recoverable from reinsurers. Since manufacturers and retailers often borrow to fund their operations, their liabilities typically include substantial amounts for accounts payable and long-term debt. An insurer's liabilities typically include loss reserves, loss adjustment expenses, and unearned premiums.

21) What is a statement of income (or income statement)?

The income statement records revenues from sales and the costs of making those sales, as well as other expenses, such as taxes, and sources of profit, such as investments.

22) What are other names for the income statement?

The income statement may also be referred to as (a) a statement of earnings, (b) a profit and loss (P&L) statement, or (c) a statement of operations.

23) Briefly describe the information found on an insurer's statement of income.

An insurer's statement of income shows its underwriting income, net investment income, net income before deductions, and net income. Underwriting income is determined as the insurer's earned premiums less the sum of the insurer's incurred losses, loss adjustment expenses (LAE), and other underwriting expenses. This is the insurer's underwriting profit or loss. Net investment income is investment income minus investment losses and certain investment-related expenses. Net income before deductions is the sum of the underwriting profit or loss and net investment gain or loss. Net income is calculated as net income before deductions, less income taxes and dividends paid to policyholders.

24) What is the statement of cash flows?

The statement of cash flows is a financial statement that reconciles the amount of cash an organization has at the end of a period with the amount it had at the beginning of that same period by documenting the sources and uses of cash during the period.

25) What types of activities does the statement of cash flows focus on?

It focuses on three general types of activities: (a) operations, (b) investments, and (c) financing.

26) What is the statement of changes in owners' equity?

The statement of changes in owners' equity shows any investments in the organization made by owners, including shareholders, and any disbursements made to them over a given period.

27) What are other names for the statement of changes in owners' equity?

The statement of changes in owners' equity may also be referred to as (a) statement of changes in capital stock or (b) the statement of changes in retained earnings.

28) What are the important considerations when compiling financial statements?

When compiling financial statements, it is important to determine how revenues and expenses will be recognized.

29) Define revenues and expenses.

Revenues are the funds organizations receive from the sale of products or the provision of services. It increases owners' equity.

Expenses are costs incurred to generate revenues. It decreases owners' equity.

30) Explain the GAAP principle of revenue recognition and how it is reflected in property and casualty insurance.

The GAAP principle of revenue recognition specifies that revenue is recognized at the time that an exchange is made or a service is provided, rather than when payment is received. In property and casualty insurance, the principal of revenue recognition is reflected in the fact that premiums are recognized over the policy period as the insurance protection outlined in the policy is provided.

31) Explain the GAAP matching principle. Provide an example.

Under the GAAP matching principle, when determining net income for a particular period, revenues for that period are matched with the expenses that produced them. For example, a wholesaler purchases $100,000 in goods in the first quarter of the year. No sales are made until the second quarter of the year. During the second quarter of the year, all the goods were sold for $200,000. Since the revenue of $200,000 was recognized in the second quarter, the associated $100,000 cost of purchasing the inventory should be matched and included as an expense in the second quarter income statement, despite the actual purchase being made in the first quarter.

32) How does the matching principle work when an organization's assets have a useful life of many years? What is an example of such an asset?

An example of an asset with a long useful life is an organization's building and equipment. For these assets, to match expenses with associated revenues, the purchase price would be expensed over the item's life through depreciation or amortization.

33) Provide an example of how an asset would be depreciated.

Let's take a piece of computing equipment that was purchased for $150,000. It is anticipated to remain operational for 15 years. Under depreciation, it could be expensed at a rate of $10,000 per year.

34) What does the accounting principle of conservatism require when estimates are used?

Depreciation usually involves estimates that result in income statements that provide only an approximation of net income. In these situations, the accounting principle of conservatism requires that financial statements should reflect the lowest reasonable net income for the period.

35) What happens when an organization's expenses cannot be directly linked or matched to revenues? Provide an example of when this might occur.

An example of this situation occurs when an insurer contracts the services of an office cleaning company. This expense cannot be matched directly to premium revenues. Under these circumstances, expenses are typically recognized when they are incurred. While GAAP provides rules and guidelines, accounting also requires the exercise of reasonable judgment.

36) How does the insurance industry differ from other industries?

- Rather than sell a product or service, insurers assume the financial risks of their insureds.
- The cost of future claims on a particular policy is unknown when the policy is sold.
- Insurers price their products based on estimates of future losses rather than known costs.
- Insurers' principal, statutory, and regulatory obligations are to their policyholders.

37) Why do insurers have a greater risk of becoming insolvent than other organizations?

Insurers have a greater potential for becoming insolvent than other organizations because of the uncertainties associated with the provision and pricing of insurance. This can leave them unable to meet their obligations to insureds and claimants.

38) Provide some examples of how an insurer can become insolvent.

An insurer's financial strength can be impaired if the company inadvertently underprices its products or intentionally charges inadequate rates to gain market share. Insolvency can occur if an insurer faces unanticipated loss frequency and severity with insufficient loss and LAE reserves or inadequate reinsurance provisions.

39) How did statutory accounting principles develop?

Historically, insurer insolvency left policyholders without the required protection, which was considered contrary to the public interest. Often, alternative coverage was unavailable, leaving those who subsequently suffered losses in financial ruin. Statutory accounting principles grew out of the need to help ensure the ongoing solvency of insurance carriers. SAP are outlined by the NAIC and so, may vary from jurisdiction to jurisdiction.

40) What are some of the fundamental differences between SAP and GAAP?

Fundamental differences exist between SAP and GAAP in regard to (a) the assumptions made, (b) the treatment of assets, and (c) the recognition of some expenses. These differences exist because GAAP focuses on measuring earnings, while SAP's objective is to ensure solvency.

41) Briefly describe what assumptions are made in SAP and how it differs from GAAP.

With GAAP, the accounting approach used is the going-concern assumption. It recognizes the value of the income stream that an organization will generate. With SAP, the accounting approach used is the liquidation assumption. It only recognizes the sale or liquidation value of an organization's assets.

42) Briefly describe how assets are treated in SAP and how they differ from GAAP.

With GAAP, all of an organization's assets are listed on the balance sheet.

With SAP, some types of assets must be excluded from an insurer's balance sheet. These excluded assets are referred to as non-admitted assets, which are usually illiquid, or their inclusion is disallowed by statute.

43) Briefly describe how expenses are recognized in SAP and how it differs from GAAP.

Under GAAP, the matching principle applies, and policy acquisition costs are recognized as an expense over the policy term, just as premiums are earned over the policy term.

With SAP, policy acquisition costs must be fully recognized as an expense at the point of incurring them.

44) **What effect do the differences between SAP and GAAP have on the financial statements generated by an insurer?**

Since not all assets can be included in SAP, this results in a more conservative estimate of the policyholder's surplus than under GAAP. By recognizing policy acquisition costs when a policy is sold, but earning premiums over the policy term under SAP, this results in a more conservative handling of insurer income than GAAP.

45) **Give examples of non-admitted assets.**

Non-admitted assets include (a) premiums overdue by 90 days or more, (b) furniture, and (c) office equipment.

46) **What are policy acquisition costs? Give examples.**

Policy acquisition costs are those costs that arise directly out of the provision of insurance coverage. General expenses, such as lease and mortgage payments, are not considered policy acquisition costs. Examples include (a) sales commission paid to agents and brokers, (b) the cost of printing and mailing policies to policyholders, and (c) state premium taxes.

47) **What are the two types of data reporting regulations to which insurers are subject?**

They are (a) financial data reporting and (b) statistical data reporting regulations.

48) **State the purpose served by each of the two types of data reported.**

The data insurers provide to regulators form the basis for evaluating insurer solvency, assessing the relationships between rates and coverages, and monitoring market trends. Financial data are used primarily for solvency evaluation, while statistical data are used primarily for evaluation of the appropriateness of rates and the availability of adequate insurance.

49) **What is the source of financial and statistical data?**

Financial and statistical data flow from the same source -- individual premium and loss transactions.

50) **What is the Annual Statement?**

The Annual Statement form is produced and maintained by the NAIC. It is used for financial data reporting. All insurers licensed to write business in a given jurisdiction are required to submit this report to the state's insurance regulator each year. Its purpose is to assist regulators in evaluating insurers' solvency and determining when action may be necessary to protect the interests of insurers' policyholders.

51) How is the financial data in the Annual Statement reported?

The data is reported by jurisdiction and by line of insurance (e.g., private passenger automobile or general liability).

52) How are statistical data reported to the regulators?

For most regulators, statistical data are reported by designated statistical agents who collect them from insurers and compile them in formats specified by the regulator. These compilations are referred to as statistical filings. Statistical data are collected through statistical plans, which provide specific instructions on the manner in which premium and loss transactions are to be reported to statistical agents.

53) What is the difference between unit transaction coding and summary reporting in statistical data reporting?

Unit transaction coding requires a statistical record for any policy transaction. As a result, a single policy may have multiple statistical records associated with it. Summary reporting allows some transactions to be combined. However, this method does not typically provide sufficient granularity for effective ratemaking.

54) Provide a few examples of unit transaction coding in statistical data reporting.

If a car is added to a personal automobile policy or the collision deductible is changed, a separate statistical premium record is required. For losses, a separate record is coded for each reserve, each reserve adjustment, each claim payment, and each allocated adjustment expense per claimant by coverage.

55) List a few differences between financial and statistical data.

- Financial data reported are more summarized than statistical data.
- Financial data is typically compiled on a calendar-year basis, while statistical data is usually compiled on an accident-year and/or policy-year basis.
- Statistical data is dynamic, whereas financial data is, in general, static.

56) **Why is it important that data managers understand the differences between financial and statistical reporting, as well as the differences between SAP and GAAP?**

This is because data managers are responsible for determining which data needs to be collected to meet all of an insurer's reporting obligations.

57) **What are the objectives of the data manager as they relate to insurance accounting?**

The data manager needs to ensure that, for each type of reporting, the correct data appears in the correct lines of each form. The data manager needs to identify and implement appropriate measures to ensure that both financial and statistical data are as complete and accurate as possible and that the two types of data can be reconciled.

58) **How does the data manager achieve these objectives as it relates to insurance accounting?**

To achieve these objectives, the data manager must effectively use metadata and thoroughly document the data lineage.

59) **What are the components of the NAIC Annual Statement?**

The NAIC Annual Statement contains the following items:

- jurat page
- balance sheet
- income statement
- cash flow statement
- special schedules and supplements.

60) **Briefly describe the individual components of the NAIC Annual Statement.**

The jurat page provides general information about the insurance company, including contact details and the names of its directors and officers. The balance sheet lists the organization's assets, nonadmitted assets, and net admitted assets, along with an overview of its investments. The insurer's liabilities are also listed. The income statement presents information about the insurer's net income from investments and underwriting. The cash flow statement illustrates the organization's cash flows from operations, investment, and financing. The special schedules and supplements contain more detailed information.

61) **List a few examples of the special schedules and supplements found in the NAIC Annual Statement.**

- The Underwriting and Investment Exhibit.
- The Exhibit of Net Investment Income and Exhibit of Capital Gains (Losses).
- The Notes of Financial Statements.
- The General Interrogatories.
- The Five Year Historical Data Summary.
- The Exhibit of Premiums and Losses.
- Schedule F.
- Schedule H.
- Schedule P.
- Schedule T.
- Schedule Y.
- The Insurance Expense Exhibit.
- Schedule D.

62) **In general, how does the NAIC treat loss adjustment expenses for reporting purposes?**

For many reporting purposes, loss adjustment expenses are categorized as allocated and unallocated. Expenses that can be directly linked to a particular claim, such as lawyers' fees in a liability claim, are referred to as allocated loss adjustment expenses (ALAE). Other expenses that cannot be directly related to a particular claim, such as claims adjusters' salaries, are often referred to as unallocated loss adjustment expenses (ULAE).

63) **When and how did the NAIC's treatment of loss adjustment expenses change for statutory financial reporting?**

In 1998, the NAIC changed how loss adjustment expenses (LAE) were categorized for statutory financial reporting. LAE was re-categorized as either defense and cost containment (DCC) expenses or adjusting and other (A&O) expenses.

64) **Define defense and cost containment (DCC) expenses. Provide some examples.**

Defense and cost-containment expenses are related to defending claims or managing the costs associated with them. Some examples include fees for lawyers, private investigators, or fraud investigators if the insurer is defending against a claim. Other examples include medical record reviews, rehabilitation services, or the cost of medical examinations in accident insurance claims.

Define adjusting and other (A&O) expenses. Provide some examples.

Adjusting and other expenses are the remaining LAE that are not directly related to defense and cost containment. Some examples would include the costs associated with adjusting and paying claims, such as claims adjusters' salaries.

65) What do data managers involved in the generation of these reports need to be aware of?

Data managers involved in the creation or compilation of internal, external or statutory reports, whether statistical or financial, need to be aware of how required data elements are defined. This is because definitions used at the jurisdictional level may differ from those of the NAIC.

66) In what areas does effective data management add value?

Effective data management adds value in the areas of (a) statutory and financial accounting, (b) premium and loss transaction booking, (c) control of collections, (d) data collection, storage, and dispersal, (e) strategic planning, and (f) compliance.

67) How does the data manager add value in the statutory and financial accounting arena?

Data managers establish controls that ensure the accuracy of statutory, financial, and statistical reporting. They identify ways to capture and share the required data across systems and applications. Additionally, they help to identify and support the development of controls to meet solvency requirements.

68) How does the data manager add value in the premium and loss transaction booking arena?

Data managers help define and establish internal data standards and controls to enhance and maintain the accuracy of premium and loss data. They help ensure that data is reconciled as it passes from system to system or from application to application. They facilitate data exchange with others, including insureds, reinsurers, and vendors.

69) How does the data manager add value in the control of collections?

Data managers work to ensure that data are controlled and reconcilable at the vendor, producer, and insured levels. They also ensure that the data can be accessed quickly and easily. They ensure that receivables and collections are balanced, and that payables and payments are balanced.

70) How does the data manager add value in the collection, storage, and dispersal of data?

Data managers reduce the cost of data collection, storage and dispersal by assisting in the identification of redundant systems, applications and functions. They recommend consolidations and improvements. They maintain data standards that simplify communications between systems and applications.

71) How does the data manager add value in the strategic planning arena?

Data managers influence strategic planning by promoting the recognition of data as a significant asset. They assist management in maximizing the value of data to the organization. In support of this, data managers define data requirements, promote the use of industry standards, develop internal standards and quality controls, and help identify ways to monitor the organization's actual performance against its objectives.

72) How does the data manager add value in the compliance arena?

Data managers work with regulators, workers' compensation administrators, advisory organizations, research organizations, standards organizations, and other industry groups to ensure that statutory, financial, and statistical reporting, as well as other compliance recommendations, are achievable. They keep current with the requirements set by regulators and specify ways to meet them. Finally, they implement controls to access financial systems data and release data only to authorized personnel, to meet privacy and confidentiality requirements.

Insurance Regulation: History, Purpose, and Standards

Educational Objectives

Upon completion of this assignment, you should be able to:

1. Describe the major events in the evolution of property-liability insurance that led to regulatory oversight in insurance.
2. Describe the four major responsibilities of insurance regulators with respect to overseeing the operations of property and casualty insurers.
3. Explain how federal legislation since the late 1990s has affected insurance companies.
4. Compare insurance regulation under an optional federal charter with state regulation.
5. Explain the role of the National Association of Insurance Commissioners (NAIC) in insurance regulation and describe the international efforts of the NAIC.
6. Explain the importance of the NAIC Model Regulation to Require Reporting of Statistical Data by Property and Casualty Insurance Companies and the NAIC Statistical Handbook of Data Available to Insurance Regulators.
7. Describe the purpose of an insurer solvency exam, and how one is performed.
8. Describe the purpose and process of insurer conservation, rehabilitation, and liquidation.
9. Describe the International Association of Industrial Accident Boards and Commissions (IAIABC).
10. Identify the major international insurance standards organizations.

For each assignment, define or describe each of the Key Terms and Concepts and answer each of the Review and Discussion Questions.

Key Terms and Concepts

Admitted insurer:

Alien insurers:

Anti-compact laws:

Antitrust laws:

Asset risk:

Captive insurer:

Conservator:

Conservation:

Covered products:

Domicile:

Fair Access to Insurance Requirements (FAIR) programs:

Fixed capital requirements:

Foreign insurer:

Full-scope examination:

Group captive:

Guarantee fund:

Limited-scope examinations:

Liquidation:

Non-admitted insurers:

Receiver:

Rehabilitation:

Residual markets:

Risk-based capital (RBC) model:

Surplus lines market:

Underwriting risk:

Zone examination or association examinations:

Review Questions

1) What were some of the approaches to insurance regulation taken by states prior to 1850?

2) What is the ongoing debate in the U.S. regarding insurance regulation?

3) List the historical events that helped shape the current regulatory environment.

4) What was the impact of the Paul vs. Virginia decision on insurance regulation?

5) What role did the National Insurance Convention play in shaping the current regulatory environment?

6) What was the impact of the Sherman Antitrust Act on insurance regulation?

7) Describe the "underwriting cycle".

8) How did insurers attempt to break the "underwriting cycle"?

9) What was the purpose of the Clayton Antitrust Act?

10) What was the result of the Federal Trade Commission Act?

11) What was the impact of the United States vs. South-Eastern Underwriters Association (SEUA) decision on insurance regulation?

12) What was the impact of the McCarran-Ferguson Act on insurance regulation?

13) What is the insurers' limited exemption from federal antitrust laws under the McCarran-Ferguson Act and what does it allow an insurer to do?

14) What constitutes the "business of insurance" as it relates to the limited antitrust exemption?

15) What was the impact of the All-Industry Rating Bills on insurance regulation?

16) Why was the National Commission on State Workmen's Compensation Laws created?

17) What were the results of the National Commission on State Workmen's Compensation Laws?

18) List the four primary areas of responsibility of state regulators.

19) What some of the mechanisms that have been developed by the NAIC to address insurer solvency?

20) Why was the Early Warning Test program developed?

21) How do regulators monitor insurers' financial strength?

22) What is the purpose of the accreditation program developed by the NAIC?

23) How is rate regulation accomplished?

24) Explain why insurance policy wording is regulated.

25) How is insurance policy wording regulated?

26) List some of the approaches that have been developed by regulators to address the issues of availability and affordability of insurance.

27) Describe the state Fair Access to Insurance Requirements (FAIR) programs.

28) What are residual markets and why do they exist?

29) Describe the two forms of captives.

30) Differentiate between an admitted and nonadmitted insurer.

31) Define and describe how the surplus lines market works.

32) List two programs created by the federal government to address the issues of availability and affordability of insurance.

33) What does the National Flood Insurance Program achieve?

34) What is the Federal Crop Insurance Corporation?

35) What does market conduct focus on?

36) List the acts that regulators have developed to address market conduct concerns.

37) Provide some examples of what the Unfair Trade Practices Act prohibits and/or stipulates.

38) Provide some examples of unfair claim settlement practices.

39) List some federal legislation that has impacted insurers since 1990.

40) Briefly describe the main points of the Health Insurance Portability and Accountability Act.

41) What was the impact of HIPAA on insurers?

42) State the purpose of the Gramm-Leach-Bliley Act and name the three principal parts.

43) Describe the Financial Privacy Rule of the Gramm-Leach-Bliley Act.

44) Describe the Safeguards Rule of the Gramm-Leach-Bliley Act.

45) Describe the Pretexting Provisions of the Gramm-Leach-Bliley Act.

46) Briefly describe what the USA PATRIOT Act accomplished.

47) What is the Bank Secrecy Act?

48) What is the impact of the USA PATRIOT Act on insurers?

49) In the context of the Bank Secrecy Act, define "covered products" and provide a few examples.

50) What are Specially Designated Nationals?

51) What led to the Sarbanes-Oxley Act?

52) What is the purpose of the Sarbanes-Oxley Act and how is that purpose achieved?

53) What is the impact of the Sarbanes-Oxley Act on insurers?

54) What is the purpose of the Terrorism Risk Insurance Act (TRIA)?

55) How does TRIA achieve its purpose?

56) What precipitated the Dodd-Frank Act?

57) What is the impact of the Dodd-Frank Act on insurers?

58) List the advantages of state regulation.

59) List the disadvantages of state regulation.

60) List the advantages of federal regulation.

61) List the disadvantages of federal regulation.

62) State the NAIC's mission.

63) Name one way in which the NAIC fulfills its mission.

64) Briefly describe the function of the NAIC's Financial Regulation Standards Accreditation Committee (FRSAC).

65) What role does the NAIC's Support and Services office play?

66) Describe the role of the NAIC Government Relations Office.

67) What is the mission of the NAIC's International Insurance Relations Committee?

68) Describe the purpose of the NAIC's Securities Valuation Office (SVO).

69) What is a key fact to remember regarding the designations made by the NAIC's Securities Valuation Office?

70) Name the two most important NAIC documents to property and casualty data managers.

71) What is the purpose of the NAIC Model Regulation to Require Reporting of Statistical Data by Property and Casualty Insurance Companies?

72) List the areas the model regulation touches upon.

73) Who maintains the Statistical Handbook and how does it maintain it?

74) What is the focus of the Statistical Handbook?

75) Briefly describe the introductory section of the Statistical Handbook.

76) Briefly describe the second section of the Statistical Handbook.

77) Briefly describe the third section of the Statistical Handbook.

78) List the types of insurance coverage subject to statistical data reporting as prescribed by the Statistical Handbook.

79) What is the NAIC Insurance Regulatory Information System (IRIS)?

80) What purpose does the IRIS serve?

81) Briefly describe how the IRIS works to achieve its purpose.

82) What is the focus of the IRIS ratios?

83) What is the focus of the FAST ratios?

84) Describe the steps of a solvency exam.

85) Describe fixed capital requirements.

86) What is a disadvantage of the fixed capital requirements method for preventing insolvency?

87) What is the risk-based capital model?

88) How does the risk-based capital model differ from fixed capital requirements?

89) Define asset risk, underwriting risk, and other risks as they relate to the RBC model.

90) Under the Risk-Based Capital for Insurers Model Act, what are the available options when minimum capital requirements are not met?

91) What is the purpose of the Financial Analysis Handbook?

92) How often are regulators required to review an insurer's financial condition?

93) What are the two types of examinations that are performed by regulators?

94) What is an Own Risk and Solvency Assessment (ORSA)?

95) Describe how insurer insolvencies are handled.

96) What options are available to a receiver when dealing with financially troubled insurers?

97) What happens to existing policies when an insurer is liquidated?

98) What is the International Association of Industrial Accident Boards and Commissions (IAIABC) and its purpose?

99) Name some of the international insurance organizations.

Answers to Assignment 8 Questions

NOTE: These answers are provided to give students a basic understanding of acceptable types of responses. They are often not the only valid answers and are not intended to provide an exhaustive response to the questions.

Key Terms and Concepts

Admitted insurer: An admitted insurer is one that is licensed or incorporated to write business in the insured's home state.

Alien insurers: Insurers domiciled outside the United States.

Anti-compact laws: Laws prohibiting insurers from forming associations to set or control rates.

Antitrust laws: Antitrust laws prohibit agreements, associations, or practices that restrain trade or obstruct open competition.

Asset risk: The risk that assets (of the insurer), for example, investments, will lose value.

Captive insurer: A captive insurer is one that is owned and controlled by its insureds.

- Single-parent captive insurer, a type of captive insurer where the parent company owns the captive and the captive insures the parent company and its subsidiaries.
- Group captive insurer, a type of captive insurer where the owner is a group of companies, typically from within the same industry.

Conservator: In the case of an insolvent insurer, the person or organization selected to manage the affairs of a bankrupt individual or organization and to receive official documents is referred to as the conservator.

Conservation: One option for dealing with a financially troubled insurer is to preserve the insurer's assets during the period needed to evaluate the situation and determine the best course of action.

Covered products: Insurance products that have a savings or cash value, such as some life insurance policies and annuities.

Domicile: The state in which an insurer is incorporated.

Fair Access to Insurance Requirements (FAIR) programs: State-mandated programs that provide fair access to insurance for individuals who have trouble obtaining insurance, possibly due to the insurers considering them high risk. The FAIR plan is a "shared market" plan.

Fixed capital requirements: The minimum amounts of capital a licensed insurer must have in order to do business in a jurisdiction, ensuring insurers have sufficient money and assets to support their underwriting activities.

Foreign insurer: A foreign insurer is one that is incorporated (or domiciled) in the United States but outside the state in which the insurance is written.

Full-scope examination: A detailed review of an insurer's overall financial strength and operations performed by insurance departments to more accurately identify insurers and/or holding company systems experiencing financial problems or to identify prospective risks that pose the greatest potential for developing financial problems.

Guarantee fund: A state fund generally funded by assessments collected from all insurers licensed in the state. The Guarantee Fund pays claims of insolvent insurers.

Limited-scope examinations: Limited-scope, or targeted, examinations focus on specific areas or issues of an insurer's overall financial strength and operations conducted by insurance departments to more accurately identify insurers and/or holding company systems experiencing financial problems or to identify prospective risks that pose the greatest potential for developing financial problems.

Liquidation: The regulatory process by which the regulator or receiver liquidates the insurer's assets and distributes the proceeds to policyholders and other creditors according to a system of priorities set out in state law.

Non-admitted insurers: Insurers that are not licensed to do business in the insured's home state. They are not regulated in the state and do not contribute to the State Guaranty Fund, which protects policyholders from the insolvency of its insurance carrier.

Receiver: A person or organization selected to manage the affairs of a bankrupt individual or organization.

Rehabilitation: The regulatory process by which the regulator takes control of the insurer's assets under court supervision, develops a rehabilitation plan that it submits to the court for approval, and, if it receives a rehabilitation order, the receiver is responsible for implementing the requirements set out in the rehabilitation order.

Residual markets: An insurance pool or other mechanism established by a jurisdiction to provide insurance for individuals who cannot obtain coverage in the standard or voluntary market is called a residual market.

Risk-based capital (RBC) model: The risk-based capital (RBC) model is an approach regulators use to determine an insurer's minimum capital requirements based on a formula that depends on an insurer's individual risk profile.

Surplus lines market: A market in which applicants who are unable to obtain insurance coverage from admitted insurers can purchase it from non-admitted insurers.

Underwriting risk: Underwriting risk measures the volatility of loss experience across different coverages and lines of business.

Zone examination or association examinations: A zone examination (also referred to as an association examination) is one in which the regulator of the state in which the insurer is domiciled undertakes the financial evaluation and invites the participation of examiners from the other zones in which the insurer operates. Special association examination – An examination conducted by the NAIC if the examination by a jurisdiction is inadequate, has not been scheduled by the jurisdiction when IRIS or other sources indicate there is a need, or if a state in which the insurer is licensed requests it.

Review Questions

1) What were some of the approaches to insurance regulation taken by states prior to 1850?

Prior to 1850, states varied in their approach to insurance regulation. Some states passed protectionist laws prohibiting insurers incorporated in another country from writing business within the state. Some states charged foreign insurers a 10% premium tax on business written in their state.

2) What is the ongoing debate in the U.S. regarding insurance regulation?

As the U.S. insurance industry grew, an ongoing debate emerged over whether insurance should fall under state or federal control.

3) List the historical events that helped shape the current regulatory environment.

- Paul vs. Virginia decision in 1869.
- National Insurance Convention in 1871.
- The Sherman Antitrust Act of 1890.
- The Clayton Antitrust Act of 1914.
- The Federal Trade Commission Act of 1914.
- United States vs. South-Eastern Underwriters Association decision in 1944.
- McCarran-Ferguson Act in 1945.
- All-Industry Rating Bills.
- The National Commission on State Workmen's Compensation Laws of 1972.

4) What was the impact of the Paul vs. Virginia decision on insurance regulation?

As a result of Paul vs. Virginia, the U.S. Supreme Court declared that insurance was not considered interstate commerce. This meant that states retained regulatory control over the business of insurance.

5) What role did the National Insurance Convention play in shaping the current regulatory environment?

The National Insurance Convention (NIC) was formed in 1871 by regulators who recognized the challenges faced by insurers seeking to maintain licenses to sell coverage in multiple states, as each state regulated the business of insurance differently. These challenges increased the insurers' costs, which, in turn, increased the rates charged to policyholders. The NIC evolved into the National Commission of Insurance Commissioners (NCIC) and then later became the National Association of Insurance Commissioners (NAIC). Through the NAIC, state insurance regulators establish standards and best practices, conduct peer review, and coordinate their regulatory oversight.

6) What was the impact of the Sherman Antitrust Act on insurance regulation?

Because insurance was not considered interstate commerce, the Sherman Antitrust Act did not apply directly to insurers. However, some states did pass antitrust laws and by 1912, twenty-three states had passed anitcompact laws that prohibited insurers from forming associations for the purposes of setting or controlling rates. Regulators recognized that applying antitrust laws to insurance operations was problematic. The states eventually came to support the use of rating bureaus in order to help ensure rate adequacy and stability. These rating bureaus were the precursor to today's insurer advisory organizations.

7) Describe the "underwriting cycle".

In an underwriting cycle, the desire to increase market share drives some insurers to relax underwriting standards and lower rates. To remain competitive, other insurers follow suit, and consumers find insurance coverage easy to obtain at acceptable premiums. This is referred to as a "soft market". However, ultimately, this inadequate pricing results in underwriting losses and even insurer insolvencies. Insurers respond by tightening underwriting standards and increasing rates. Consumers may find coverage difficult to obtain at an affordable price. This is referred to as a "hard market".

8) How did insurers attempt to break the "underwriting cycle"?

To attempt to break the underwriting cycle, insurers organized. This allowed the sharing of premium and loss data, helping ensure rate adequacy. In turn, this created stability within the insurance market and reduced the risk of insurer insolvencies.

9) What was the purpose of the Clayton Antitrust Act?

The Clayton Antitrust Act served to proscribe practices not addressed under the Sherman Antitrust Act. Section 7 of the Clayton Act prohibited mergers and acquisitions that may substantially lessen competition or tend to create a monopoly.

10) What was the result of the Federal Trade Commission Act?

Passed in 1914, the Federal Trade Commission Act created the U.S. Federal Trade Commission (FTC), which is a bipartisan federal agency with a unique dual mission to protect consumers and promote competition. The Federal Trade Commission Act also proscribes "unfair methods of competition" and "unfair or deceptive acts or practices."

11) What was the impact of the United States vs. South-Eastern Underwriters Association (SEUA) decision on insurance regulation?

The effect of the Supreme Court's decision in the SEUA case was that the Sherman Act, the Clayton Act, and the FTC Act all applied to the insurance industry. The implications for the insurance industry were significant. Many state insurance regulators believed that some forms of cooperation were necessary within the industry, particularly pooling and sharing statistical data for ratemaking. The National Association of Insurance Commissioners (NAIC) recommended that the industry press Congress to amend the Commerce Clause of the Constitution, as well as the Sherman Act, the Clayton Act, and the FTC Act, to create special provisions for the insurance industry.

12) What was the impact of the McCarran-Ferguson Act on insurance regulation?

The McCarran-Ferguson Act allows states to regulate and tax foreign insurers that write business within their jurisdictions. Additionally, it provides the industry with a limited exemption from federal antitrust laws, provided that the states have antitrust and unfair trade practices laws in place. Under the Act's provisions, Congress retains the right to pass laws relating to the business of insurance or to modify existing laws so they apply to that business. In these situations, federal law would supersede any conflicting state law.

13) What is the insurer's limited exemption from federal antitrust laws under the McCarran-Ferguson Act, and what does it allow an insurer to do?

The insurers' limited exemption applies only to the "business of insurance". It allows insurers to pool historical loss data to develop more actuarially sound rates and jointly develop policy forms.

14) What constitutes the "business of insurance" as it relates to the limited antitrust exemption?

The Supreme Court devised a three-part test to determine whether an activity constitutes the business of insurance. The activity must involve underwriting risk, a contract between the insurer and the insured, and be unique to the insurance industry.

15) What was the impact of the All-Industry Rating Bills on insurance regulation?

After the enactment of the McCarran-Ferguson Act, the All-Industry Insurance Committee formed by the NAIC was tasked with determining the state regulations necessary to satisfy the requirements set forth by the act. The result was the development and adoption of two rate regulation model acts in 1945. One was for property insurance and the other for casualty insurance. These were among the first model laws developed by the NAIC with the intent of promoting uniform insurance regulation across all states.

16) Why was the National Commission on State Workmen's Compensation Laws created?

Prior to the appointment of a National Commission on State Workmen's Compensation Laws, compensation and benefit levels provided to injured workers varied from state to state. The commission examined the adequacy of state workers' compensation provisions.

17) What were the results of the National Commission on State Workmen's Compensation Laws?

The commission's report included 19 recommendations and the proposal that the federal government should assume responsibility for workers' compensation in any state that did not implement those recommendations by the set deadline. To avoid federalization of workers' compensation, the states passed laws that broadened coverage, improved wage-loss benefits, enhanced medical and rehabilitation coverage, and improved workplace safety.

18) List the four primary areas of responsibility of state regulators.

- Insurer solvency.
- Rates and products.
- Market structure and performance (availability and affordability).
- Market conduct.

19) What are some of the mechanisms that the NAIC has developed to address insurer solvency?

The NAIC adopted the Post-Assessment Property and Business Insurance Guarantee Association Model Act, which created a mechanism for addressing insurer insolvencies through guarantee funds. Additionally, the NAIC developed and implemented the Early Warning Tests program (later known as the Insurance Regulatory Information System) to evaluate an insurer's financial strength and detect those that were in or likely to be in financial difficulty. Most recently, the NAIC has launched an accreditation program to develop and maintain standards to promote effective insurance company financial solvency regulation.

20) Why was the Early Warning Test program developed?

It was designed to help regulators require an insurer to take corrective action before it actually becomes insolvent. This had two benefits: (1) it helped to prevent insurer insolvencies, and (2) it helped control the state guarantee assessments insurers were required to pay.

21) How do regulators monitor insurers' financial strength?

Regulators establish financial standards that insurers are required to meet and then monitor their performance against those standards. They review insurers' statutory financial statements. They make use of information and analysis systems, such as IRIS. They also conduct on-site field audits of insurers' financial records.

22) What is the purpose of the accreditation program developed by the NAIC?

The purpose of the accreditation program is for state insurance departments to meet baseline solvency standards, particularly with respect to the regulation of multi-state insurers.

23) How is rate regulation accomplished?

Rate regulation is accomplished in different ways depending on the line of business and jurisdiction involved. In some cases, insurers may be required to use mandatory rates developed by the state or by an authorized rating bureau. When the state does not mandate rates, there are various approaches to rate regulation, including prior-approval laws, file-and-use laws, flex-rating laws, and open-competition laws. Regardless of the type of rating laws in place, insurers are also required to collect and report specific data to state regulators for analysis to determine appropriate rate levels or to evaluate the availability of adequate coverage within a market.

24) Explain why insurance policy wording is regulated.

Insurance policies are complex documents that can be difficult for the average consumer to understand and interpret; and, in most lines, the consumer has no control over the content of the policy form.

25) How is insurance policy wording regulated?

Regulators may require the use of standard policy forms. They may require insurers to obtain regulatory approval before using any nonstandard policy wording. They may establish mandatory policy provisions or minimum coverage standards that insurers must meet. They may also require that policy forms be written so that consumers can easily understand them.

26) List some of the approaches that regulators have developed to address the issues of availability and affordability of insurance.

- Establishment of state FAIR programs to provide property insurance coverage.
- Establishment of residual markets to provide automobile liability insurance.
- Passing of laws to allow captive insurers.
- Allowing for the development of alternative insurance markets.

27) Describe the state Fair Access to Insurance Requirements (FAIR) programs.

State FAIR are insurance pools that allow otherwise unrelated insurers to collectively provide property insurance coverage. In insurance pools, a group of insurers share loss exposures that they would be unwilling or unable to cover individually. For example, in areas prone to hurricanes, such as the Atlantic and Gulf coasts, insurance pools provide windstorm coverage to commercial property owners and homeowners who would otherwise be unable to obtain it. Insurers participating in FAIR pools have access to a federal reinsurance fund.

28) What are residual markets and why do they exist?

Residual markets are mechanisms designed to provide automobile liability insurance to individuals with poor driving records who cannot obtain coverage in the standard or voluntary market. They exist because states require all vehicle owners to have automobile liability insurance.

29) Describe the two forms of captives.

The two forms of captives are single-parent and group. In a single-parent captive, the parent company owns the captive, which insures the parent company and its subsidiaries. In a group captive, the owner is a group of companies, typically from within the same industry.

30) Differentiate between an admitted and nonadmitted insurer.

An admitted insurer is licensed to write business in the insured's home state. Insurers that are not licensed to do business in the insured's home state are referred to as nonadmitted insurers.

31) Define and describe how the surplus lines market works.

The surplus lines market is a market in which applicants who are unable to obtain insurance coverage from admitted insurers can purchase it from nonadmitted insurers. Surplus lines insurance transactions must be conducted through specially licensed surplus lines producers. Surplus lines producers are typically required to demonstrate that a risk has been declined by admitted insurers.

32) List two programs created by the federal government to address the issues of availability and affordability of insurance.

- The National Flood Insurance Program (NFIP).
- The Federal Crop Insurance Corporation (FCIC).

33) What does the National Flood Insurance Program achieve?

Most property insurance policies exclude coverage for damage caused by flooding because a flood loss could be catastrophic for a single insurer, and the required premium would be unaffordable for many insureds. In areas prone to flooding, the federal government provides flood coverage through the National Flood Insurance Program.

34) What is the Federal Crop Insurance Corporation?

The Federal Crop Insurance Corporation is the mechanism through which Congress provides funding for the modern crop insurance system, helping farmers manage the risks of natural disasters and market fluctuations.

35) What does market conduct focus on?

Market conduct focuses on how insurers deal with applicants, insureds, claimants, and others.

36) List the acts that regulators have developed to address market conduct concerns.

- The Model Act Relating to Unfair Methods of Competition and Unfair Deceptive Acts and Practices in the Business of Insurance.
- The Unfair Claims Settlement Practices Act.

37) Provide some examples of what the Unfair Trade Practices Act prohibits and/or stipulates.

Insurance producers are prohibited from misrepresenting the coverage provided under a policy or rebating a portion of their sales commissions to an insured who purchases a policy. Underwriters are required to properly classify and rate risks, and to provide appropriate notice to the insured if a risk is canceled or nonrenewed.

38) Provide some examples of unfair claim settlement practices.

- Intentionally misleading a claimant about the coverage available under a policy.
- Not acknowledging claims promptly.
- Not having procedures in place to ensure that claims are investigated and settled promptly.
- Not settling legitimate claims promptly and fairly.
- Forcing claimants to sue by offering substantially less than a claim's reasonable value.
- Denying a claim without a proper investigation.
- Not affirming or denying coverage promptly after investigating a claim.
- Not providing a clear explanation of the reason a claim is denied.

39) List some federal legislation that has impacted insurers since 1990.

- Health Insurance Portability and Accountability Act (HIPAA).
- Gramm-Leach-Bliley Act.
- US PATRIOT Act.
- Sarbanes-Oxley Act.
- Terrorism Risk Insurance Act.
- Dodd-Frank Act.

40) Briefly describe the main points of the Health Insurance Portability and Accountability Act.

The Health Insurance Portability and Accountability Act (HIPAA) provides a means for individuals and families to transfer health insurance coverage if they change jobs, attempts to prevent healthcare fraud, and protects the confidentiality of personal health information (PHI).

One provision of HIPAA is the Privacy Rule, which protects all individually identifiable health information that a covered entity holds or transmits electronically, verbally, or on paper. Another provision is the Security Rule, which establishes standards for safeguarding PHI that is created, stored, used, or transmitted in electronic form (e-PHI).

41) What was the impact of HIPAA on insurers?

Because life and health insurers, workers' compensation insurers, and property and casualty insurers all obtain personal health information about insureds and/or claimants as part of the underwriting or claim settlement process, they needed to take steps to ensure compliance with HIPAA.

42) State the purpose of the Gramm-Leach-Bliley Act and name the three principal parts.

The Gramm-Leach-Bliley Act includes provisions to protect consumers' personal information. The three principal parts are the Financial Privacy Rule, the Safeguards Rule, and the Pretexting Provisions.

43) Describe the Financial Privacy Rule of the Gramm-Leach-Bliley Act.

The Financial Privacy Rule focuses on the collection and disclosure of customers' personal financial information. Under this rule, a financial institution must inform customers of the types of information it obtains about them, and with whom it intends to share that information. Additionally, it must explain a customer's right to refuse to have their personal information shared with certain third parties.

44) Describe the Safeguards Rule of the Gramm-Leach-Bliley Act.

The Safeguards Rule requires all financial institutions to develop, implement, and maintain safeguards to protect customer information. Companies are required to develop a written information security plan and complete the following activities:

- Designate An Information Security Coordinator.
- Identify And Assess Risks To Customer Information.
- Evaluate Current Safeguards' Effectiveness In Controlling Risks To Customer Information.
- Develop And Implement An Effective Safeguards Program.
- Monitor And Test The Effectiveness Of The Program Regularly.
- Require Service Providers To Implement Adequate Safeguards.
- Monitor Service Providers' Use Of Customer Information.
- Evaluate And Adjust The Security Program As Required.

45) Describe the Pretexting Provisions of the Gramm-Leach-Bliley Act.

The Pretexting Provisions are intended to protect consumers from individuals or organizations obtaining their personal financial information under false pretenses. It requires that financial institutions take precautions to verify a customer's identity before releasing any personal information to that customer.

46) Briefly describe what the USA PATRIOT Act accomplished.

The USA PATRIOT Act introduced legislative changes that expanded law enforcement agencies' surveillance and investigative powers in the United States. It also expanded and strengthened an existing law, the Bank Secrecy Act.

47) What is the Bank Secrecy Act?

The Bank Secrecy Act requires banks to verify customers' identity and monitor accounts for any suspicious activities, for example, currency transactions involving amounts of $10,000 or more, and report those transactions to the Treasury Department's Financial Crimes Enforcement Network.

48) What is the impact of the USA PATRIOT Act on insurers?

It extended the Bank Secrecy Act requirements to insurers selling "covered products" to prevent the transfer of funds to terrorists through such products. Insurers are also required to compare customer data with the Specially Designated Nationals (SDN) list.

49) In the context of the Bank Secrecy Act, define "covered products" and provide a few examples.

In this context, covered products are insurance products that have a savings value or cash value, such as some life insurance policies and annuities. An annuity is a contract under which, in exchange for a premium payment, the insurer agrees to make a series of periodic payments at some future date.

50) What are Specially Designated Nationals?

Specially Designated Nationals (SDN) are individuals and organizations with which U.S. businesses are prohibited from dealing, because they are, for example, drug traffickers or terrorists. The list of these individuals and organizations is maintained by the U.S. Treasury Department's Office of Foreign Assets Control (OFAC).

51) What led to the Sarbanes-Oxley Act?

The Sarbanes-Oxley Act was enacted following several high-profile bankruptcies of large organizations that revealed accounting fraud.

52) What is the purpose of the Sarbanes-Oxley Act and how is that purpose achieved?

The purpose of the Sarbanes-Oxley Act is to combat accounting fraud. The Act requires publicly traded companies to maintain adequate controls to ensure the accuracy, completeness, and integrity of their financial reporting. Executives of publicly traded companies are personally responsible for certifying that the organization's financial statements are complete and accurate. Additionally, executives are responsible for ensuring that policies and procedures are in place to ensure that both financial and nonfinancial data are compiled, tested for quality and accuracy, and reviewed by management before being released to external parties.

53) What is the impact of the Sarbanes-Oxley Act on insurers?

For some time, insurers have been required to complete and submit the NAIC Annual Statement, certified by executives, to state insurance departments. So, this requirement in the Act does not represent much of a change for insurers. However, the Act stipulates penalties for executives who certify financial statements found to be inaccurate.

In some aspects, the requirements under Sarbanes-Oxley are more stringent than those imposed under previous NAIC models. As a result, the NAIC adopted the Annual Financial Reporting Model Regulation to enhance regulators' ability to monitor insurers' financial condition. This model regulation effectively imposes Sarbanes-Oxley requirements on all insurers, including those that are not publicly owned. Under the model regulation, insurers are required to have their financial statements audited by an independent certified public accountant.

54) What is the purpose of the Terrorism Risk Insurance Act (TRIA)?

Prior to the terrorist attacks of September 11, 2011, many standard commercial property insurance policies provided coverage for losses resulting from terrorism. However, afterward, terrorism coverage became difficult or impossible to obtain, particularly in high-risk areas. Recognizing that terrorism is a real and significant catastrophe exposure for property and casualty insurers, Congress passed the Terrorism Risk Insurance Act, which created a program to make terrorism coverage available.

55) How does TRIA achieve its purpose?

TRIA made any policy exclusions for damage resulting from terrorism null and void, and required all property and casualty insurers to provide terrorism coverage with terms and conditions similar to those of other covered perils. Under TRIA, Private insurers provide coverage, and the federal government shares the cost of terrorism-related losses through a formula. The Act established a program within the Treasury Department whereby the federal government essentially acts as a reinsurer.

56) What precipitated the Dodd-Frank Act?

The Dodd-Frank Act, enacted in response to the 2008 financial crisis, stipulated reforms in banking and securities.

57) What is the impact of the Dodd-Frank Act on insurers?

The act created the Federal Insurance Office (FIO). This new entity was given the authority to monitor all aspects of the insurance sector, monitor the extent to which traditionally underserved communities and consumers have access to affordable non-health insurance products, and to represent the United

States on prudential aspects of international insurance matters, including at the International Association of Insurance Supervisors.

58) List the advantages of state regulation.

- State regulatory systems are already in place and have been for over 150 years.
- State regulators are more inclined and better able to respond to local concerns and issues than a federal agency.
- There are differing exposures and resulting coverage needs for each state.
- State regulation allows insurers and regulators to respond more quickly to changing needs within the local environment.
- State regulators are able to standardize regulation and oversight through participation in the National Association of Insurance Commissioners.

59) List the disadvantages of state regulation.

- Many insurers operate nationally, and it is challenging and costly to understand and comply with the differing regulations in the various jurisdictions in which they write business.
- Critics believe that the states have not been as effective as they should have been in monitoring insurers' market conduct and investigating consumer complaints.
- By having an insurance department in every state, the insurance expertise required for effective regulation is spread too thinly.
- Some suggest that state regulators may be tempted to loosen regulatory controls or financial oversight to attract insurers to their jurisdiction.

60) List the advantages of federal regulation.

- A single set of laws and regulatory standards administered by a single body would be far more efficient.
- National standards for policy provisions and rate filings would result in significant efficiencies for insurers, and the associated cost reductions would be passed on to consumers through lower rates.
- In an increasingly global financial services marketplace, federal regulation and federal participation in international regulatory standards organizations are essential to help U.S. insurers compete globally.
- A federal regulatory body could bring together individuals with the most insurance and regulatory expertise into a single organization with greater competence.

61) List the disadvantages of federal regulation.

- Establishing a new agency would require a significant investment of time and money.
- The transition from state regulation to federal regulation would introduce uncertainty and instability within the insurance marketplace.
- Standardizing policy provisions would create a "one-size-fits-all" approach that is inappropriate to meet the diverse needs of consumers across the country.
- A centralized regulatory body would be less responsive to insurers' and consumers' needs than local agencies.

62) State the NAIC's mission.

The mission of the NAIC is to assist state insurance regulators, individually and collectively, in serving the public interest and achieving the following fundamental insurance regulatory goals in a responsive, efficient and cost effective manner, consistent with the wishes of its members to (1) protect the public interest, (2) promote competitive markets, (3) facilitate the fair and equitable treatment of insurance consumers, (4) promote the reliability, solvency and financial solidity of insurance institutions, and (5) support and improve state regulation of insurance.

63) Name one way in which the NAIC fulfills its mission.

One way the NAIC fulfills its mission is by developing and adopting model laws, regulations, and guidelines. NAIC members and staff draft the models in consultation with other stakeholders, including government staff, consumers, trade associations, and insurers. States may enact model laws and implement model regulations and guidelines as written, or they can choose to modify them. A degree of standardization in insurance regulation across all states benefits both regulators and insurers.

64) Briefly describe the function of the NAIC's Financial Regulation Standards Accreditation Committee (FRSAC).

The NAIC's Financial Regulation Standards Accreditation Committee (FRSAC) establishes a review team that examines various areas to determine whether the DOI meets the basic financial regulation standards. If the DOI meets the standards, it receives accreditation. If it does not, the FRSAC will make recommendations that the DOI can choose to implement, and then reapply for accreditation.

65) What role does the NAIC's Support and Services office play?

The staff of the NAIC's Support and Services office in Kansas City provides assistance to state DOI by offering legal assistance, providing consumer information, developing and maintaining a variety of databases, and making NAIC publications available.

66) Describe the role of the NAIC Government Relations Office.

The NAIC Government Relations Office, located in Washington, facilitates members' contact with the federal government and informs them about federal legislation with implications for DOI. Additionally, this office monitors the financial condition of insurers deemed nationally significant and works with state regulators to identify and remediate those at risk of failure.

67) What is the mission of the NAIC's International Insurance Relations Committee?

The mission of the International Insurance Relations Committee (G) is to coordinate NAIC participation in international discussions on insurance regulatory and supervisory standard-setting and to promote international cooperation. The Committee also coordinates on international insurance matters with the U.S. federal government, including the U.S. Department of the Treasury, the Federal Reserve Board, the Office of the U.S. Trade Representative (USTR), the U.S. Department of Commerce, and other federal agencies. In addition, the Committee provides an open forum for NAIC communication with U.S. interested parties and stakeholders on international insurance matters.

68) Describe the purpose of the NAIC's Securities Valuation Office (SVO).

The NAIC maintains a Securities Valuation Office (SVO) as part of its Capital Markets and Investment Analysis Office. Insurers report ownership of securities to the NAIC. The SVO conducts credit analysis of these securities to assign an NAIC designation and/or unit price. These designations and unit prices are produced solely for the benefit of NAIC members, who may use them as part of their monitoring of the financial condition of their domiciliary insurers.

69) What is a key fact to remember regarding the designations made by the NAIC's Securities Valuation Office?

Unlike the ratings of nationally recognized statistical rating organizations, Designations made by the NAIC's Securities Valuation Office are not intended to aid the investment decision making process and are therefore not suitable for use by anyone other than NAIC members.

70) Name the two most important NAIC documents for property and casualty data managers.

- The NAIC Model Regulation To Require Reporting Of Statistical Data By Property And Casualty Insurance Companies.
- The NAIC Statistical Handbook Of Data Available To Insurance Regulators, Commonly Called The Statistical Handbook.

71) What is the purpose of the NAIC Model Regulation to Require Reporting of Statistical Data by Property and Casualty Insurance Companies?

The purpose of this model regulation is to set forth the manner of reporting data by insurers to statistical agents, to prescribe reports to be submitted by statistical agents to the commissioner, and to prescribe certain conduct in connection with these reports.

72) List the areas the model regulation touches upon.

- The selection of statistical agents.
- Filing of statistical plans by statistical agents.
- Reporting of statistical experience by insurers to statistical agents.
- Statistical agents' compliance with the Statistical Handbook.
- Data screening and checking by statistical agents.
- Data screening and checking by insurers.
- Regulators' access to data.
- Protection and disclosure of data.
- Penalties for failure to comply with data reporting requirements.

73) Who maintains the Statistical Handbook and how does it maintain it?

The NAIC's Statistical Data Working Group, under the Casualty Actuarial and Statistical Task Force, maintains the Statistical Handbook. This task force monitors the Handbook's data definitions and quality standards, and reports to ensure they are appropriate for current requirements.

74) What is the focus of the Statistical Handbook?

It focuses on the collection and reporting of statistical data.

75) Briefly describe the introductory section of the Statistical Handbook.

The introductory section of the Statistical Handbook discusses the regulatory need for statistical data, differentiates between statistical data and financial data, provides some historical context for the collection and use of statistical data, discusses the role of statistical agents, and outlines the relationship between the Model Regulation and the Statistical Handbook.

76) Briefly describe the second section of the Statistical Handbook.

The second section in the Handbook discusses data quality standards and requirements for both insurers and statistical agents.

77) Briefly describe the third section of the Statistical Handbook.

The third section discusses the types of reports statistical agents are required to compile and submit. Examples of these reports are the Annual Statistical Compilations, Fast Track Monitoring Reports, and Accelerated Reports.

78) List the types of insurance coverage subject to statistical data reporting as prescribed by the Statistical Handbook.

- Commercial general liability.
- Private passenger automobile.
- Commercial automobile.
- Homeowners and mobile homes.
- Dwelling fire and allied lines.
- Commercial and farm fire and allied lines.
- Inland marine.
- Businessowners.
- Burglary and theft.
- Glass.
- Farmowners.
- Boiler and machinery.
- Medical professional liability.
- Comprehensive personal liability.
- Aircraft.
- Crop.
- Fidelity and surety.
- Mortgage guaranty.
- Municipal bond.
- Workers' compensation.

79) What is the NAIC Insurance Regulatory Information System (IRIS)?

The NAIC Insurance Regulatory Information System (IRIS) is a collection of analytical solvency tools and databases designed to provide state insurance departments with an integrated approach to screening and analyzing the financial condition of insurers operating within their respective states.

80) What purpose does the IRIS serve?

IRIS is intended to assist state insurance departments in targeting resources to those insurers in greatest need of regulatory attention.

81) Briefly describe how the IRIS works to achieve its purpose.

Financial data from insurers' NAIC Annual Statements are used to calculate a number of IRIS financial ratios. When compared to target or expected ranges, these ratios help evaluate insurers' financial performance. This information is made available to state insurance regulators. An important component of IRIS is FAST, the acronym for Financial Analysis Solvency Tools.

82) What is the focus of the IRIS ratios?

IRIS ratios focus on (1) insurers' profitability, (2) their liquidity, which is the ease with which assets can be converted to cash, (3) the adequacy of their reserves, and (4) their overall financial condition.

83) What is the focus of the FAST ratios?

The FAST ratios highlight (1) insurers' profitability, (2) their assets, (3) the yield on their investments, (4) the adequacy of their reserves, and (4) their liquidity, cash flows, and use of debt.

84) Describe the steps of a solvency exam.

The first step in a solvency exam is calculating IRIS and FAST ratios and is referred to as the statistical phase. The next step is the analytical phase. During this phase, a team of NAIC analysts reviews the data obtained and generated during the statistical phase. Based on their analysis, the team rates insurers as "Level A", "Level B", or "Reviewed, no level". Insurers rated Level A are the highest priority in terms of requiring regulatory review. Level B indicates that there are issues or concerns, but immediate review is not required. Reviewed, no level indicates that the team of analysts found no cause for concern.

85) Describe fixed capital requirements.

Fixed capital requirements are the amounts of capital established by regulators for insurers licensed to do business in a state to ensure they have sufficient funds and assets to support their underwriting activities. The amount required can vary by state. It can also vary depending on an insurer's ownership structure and the lines of business the insurer writes.

86) What is a disadvantage of the fixed capital requirements method for preventing insolvency?

Fixed capital requirements did not take into consideration an insurer's size or the types of risks it faced.

87) What is the risk-based capital model?

The risk-based capital (RBC) model was the model developed by the NAIC as a better approach to determining insurers' minimum capital requirements. Separate RBC models were developed for life insurance, property and casualty insurance, and health and fraternal insurance because of the differences among these branches of insurance.

88) How does the risk-based capital model differ from fixed capital requirements?

The risk-based capital model focuses on asset risk, underwriting risk, and other risk, whereas fixed capital requirements do not.

89) Define asset risk, underwriting risk, and other risks as they relate to the RBC model.

Asset risk is the risk that assets, such as investments that may lose value.

Underwriting risk measures the volatility of loss experience associated with different coverages and lines of business. For example, liability coverage carries more underwriting risk than automobile collision coverage.

Other risks include unusual premium growth, customer and other creditor defaults, and a reinsurer failing.

90) Under the Risk-Based Capital for Insurers Model Act, what are the available options when minimum capital requirements are not met?

There are four possibilities depending on the extent of the shortfall. First, the insurer must submit a plan to resolve the situation to the regulators. Second, the regulator examines the insurer, and the insurer submits a plan to resolve the situation. Third, the regulator is authorized, but not required, to take control of the insurer. Lastly, the regulator is required under the terms of the model act to seize control of the insurer.

91) What is the purpose of the Financial Analysis Handbook?

The purpose of the Financial Analysis Handbook is to provide a uniform risk-focused analysis approach for insurance departments to more accurately identify insurers and/or holding company systems experiencing financial problems or to identify prospective risks that pose the greatest potential for developing financial problems.

92) How often are regulators required to review an insurer's financial condition?

Regulators can review an insurer's financial condition as frequently as necessary but every insurer must be evaluated every three to five years as a minimum.

93) What are the two types of examinations that are performed by regulators?

A full-scope examination is a detailed review of an insurer's overall financial strength and operations. Limited-scope, or targeted, examinations focus on specific areas or issues.

94) What is an Own Risk and Solvency Assessment (ORSA)?

An ORSA is an internal process undertaken by an insurer or insurance group to assess the adequacy of its risk management and current and prospective solvency positions under normal and severe stress scenarios. ORSA will require insurers to analyze all reasonably foreseeable and relevant material risks (i.e., underwriting, credit, market, operational, liquidity risks, etc.) that could have an impact on an insurer's ability to meet its policyholder obligations.

95) Describe how insurer insolvencies are handled.

Insurer insolvencies are governed by state laws, which usually appoint the insurance commissioner as the insurer's receiver to manage the affairs of a bankrupt individual or organization. Receivership proceedings are commenced in court, generally in the state where the insurer is domiciled.

96) What options are available to a receiver when dealing with financially troubled insurers?

The receiver can pursue one of three forms of receivership: conservation, rehabilitation, or liquidation.

97) What happens to existing policies when an insurer is liquidated?

Existing policies owned by insureds may be canceled on the liquidation date. The receiver may transfer these policies to one or more other insurers or find another way to continue policyholders' coverage, such as through a state guaranty fund.

98) What is the International Association of Industrial Accident Boards and Commissions (IAIABC) and its purpose?

The IAIABC is a nonprofit trade association of workers' compensation jurisdictional agencies in North America. Its membership includes agencies responsible for administering and regulating workers' compensation; workers' compensation professionals, insurers, medical providers, law firms, and organizations involved in the electronic exchange of workers' compensation data. It enhances the effectiveness and efficiency of workers' compensation systems.

99) Name some of the international insurance organizations.

- The Centre for Studies in Insurance Operations (CSIO) in Canada.
- The International Association of Insurance Supervisors (IAIS).
- The European Insurance and Occupational Pensions Authority (EIOPA).
- The International Organization for Standardization (ISO).

Insurance Regulation: Data Collection Organizations

Educational Objectives

Upon completion of this assignment, you should be able to:

1. Explain the relationship between regulators and data collection organizations.
2. Explain the roles of statistical agents and advisory organizations.
3. Explain the role statistical agents play in insurance regulation.
4. Explain the reasons why state regulators issue calls for data and how these data are used.
5. Describe how data management at a data collection organization differs from that at an insurance company.
6. Describe the purpose of AIPSO and its role in the automobile residual market.
7. Describe the purpose of the Commonwealth Automobile Reinsurers (CAR).
8. Describe the purpose of the Independent Statistical Services (ISS) and provide a summary of their services.
9. Describe the purpose of ISO and provide a summary of its services.
10. Describe the purpose of the American Association of Insurance Services (AAIS) and provide a brief summary of its services.
11. Describe the purpose of the National Independent Statistical Service (NISS) and provide a brief summary of its services.
12. Describe the purpose of the National Council on Compensation Insurance (NCCI) and provide a brief summary of its services.
13. Briefly describe other workers' compensation organizations.
14. Describe the purpose of the International Association of Industrial Accident Boards and Commissions (IAIABC) and provide a summary of its services.
15. Describe the purpose of the Surety & Fidelity Association of America (SFAA).

For each assignment, define or describe each of the Key Terms and Concepts and answer each of the Review and Discussion Questions.

Key Terms and Concepts

AIPSO:

American Association of Insurance Services (AAIS):

Assigned Risk Plans:

Calls for experience:

Automobile insurance plan (AIP):

Commercial automobile insurance plan (CAIP):

Commonwealth Automobile Reinsurers (CAR):

Compensation Insurance Rating Board (CRIB):

Data collection organizations (DCO):

Delaware Compensation Rating Bureau (DCRB):

Fidelity bond:

Independent Statistical Service (ISS):

Insurance Services Office (ISO):

International Association of Industrial Accident Boards and Commissions (IAIABC):

Joint underwriting associations (JUA):

National Council on Compensation Insurance (NCCI):

National Independent Statistical Service (NISS):

New Jersey Compensation Rating and Inspection Bureau (NJCRIB):

Obligee:

Pennsylvania Compensation Rating Bureau (PCRB):

Principal:

Reinsurance facilities (RF):

Servicing carriers:

Special calls:

Surety:

Surety & Fidelity Association of America (SFAA):

Surety bond:

Suretyship:

State fund:

Workers Compensation Insurance Organizations (WCIO):

Workers Compensation Rating and Inspection Bureau of Massachusetts (WCRIBMA):

Review Questions

1) Explain the relationship between regulators and data collection organizations. [EO 1 p 9.7]

2) Explain the roles of statistical agents and advisory organizations. [EO 2 p 9.7]

3) Why do advisory organizations develop loss costs rather than rates? [EO 2 p 9.7-9.8]

4) What are the data-related differences between a statistical agent and an advisory agent? [EO 2 p9.7-9.8]

5) Why are advisory organizations advisory in nature? [EO 2, p9.8]

6) What are some additional services an advisory organization might offer? [EO 2 p 9.8]

7) What important roles do advisory organizations play for insurers, beyond regulatory reporting? [EO 2 p9.8]

8) What is the importance of data standards to the data collection and reporting process? [EO 2 p 9.8]

9) Explain the role statistical agents play in insurance regulation. [EO 3 p 9.8]

10) List the lines of insurance for which statistical agents collect data. [EO 3 p 9.8-9.9]

11) How does the use of statistical agents result in efficiencies for both regulators and insurers? [EO 3 p 9.9]

12) What are the advantages of a centralized data collection system? [EO 3 p 9.9]

13) Statistical agents provide what other service to the government at both the state and federal levels? [EO 3 p 9.9]

14) What are some of the activities a statistical agent performs to ensure regulators receive high-quality compilations? [EO 3 p 9.9]

15) Why do statistical agents provide calls for experience to the insurers reporting to them? [EO 3 p 9.9]

16) What information does a call for experience include? [EO 3 p 9.9]

17) In general, how often do statistical agents issue calls for experience? [EO 9 p 9.9]

18) What role do the statistical agent professional data managers, including statisticians and data processing analysts, play in the data collection process? {EO 3, p9.9]

19) Explain the reasons why state regulators issue calls for data and how these data are used. [EO 4 p 9.10]

20) Provide examples of situations where regulators might need additional data. [EO 4 p 9.10]

21) What role can a statistical agent play to limit the regulators' need for a special call to insurers? [EO 9 p 9.10]

22) How does the NAIC Statistical Handbook facilitate special calls? [EO 4 p 9.10]

23) How does the NAIC facilitate special calls? [EO 4 p 9.10]

24) What are some of the challenges special calls create for insurance data managers? [EO 4 p 9.10]

25) What are some other sources for information that can be used to support a regulator's need for data? [EO 4 p 9.10]

26) What is the goal of insurance data managers with respect to special calls? [EO 4 p 9.10]

27) Why do insurance data managers work closely with regulators when responding to a data call without any assistance from a DCO? [EO 4 p 9.10]

28) Why is accuracy important for data reported in a special call? [EO 4 p 9.10]

29) Describe how data management at a data collection organization differs from that at an insurance company. [EO 5 p 9.11]

30) What is the difference between insurers and DCOs with respect to confirming the accuracy of data? [EO 5 p 9.11]

31) What is the difference between insurers and DCOs with respect to the structure of data? [EO 5 p 9.11]

32) What challenges do insurers and DCOs face regarding the codes and information collected from insurers? [EO 5 p 9.11]

33) Why is system integration usually more involved for insurers than for DCO's? [EO 5 p 9.11]

34) Why might insurer and DCO systems be incompatible? [EO 5 p 9.11]

35) Statistical agents require insurers to reconcile statistical data to the insurer's Annual Statement. What is the challenge for both insurer and DCO? [EO 5 p 9.12]

36) While security is a key concern for both insurers and DCO's, what is the difference in focus? [EO 5 p 9.12]

37) Describe the fundamental difference between insurer and DCO data management. [EO 5 p 9.12]

38) What is the purpose of the automobile residual market? [EO 6 p 9.12]

39) In addition to automobile, what other lines of insurance have residual market coverage? [EO 6 p 9.12]

40) List the approaches for providing coverage in the automobile residual market. [EO 6 p 9.12]

41) How does an automobile insurance plan (AIP) work? [EO 6 p 9.12]

42) What is a servicing carrier in an automobile insurance plan? [EO 6 p 9.12]

43) How does a commercial automobile insurance plan (CAIP) work? [EO 6 p 9.13]

44) What is a joint underwriting association (JUA) and how does it operate? [EO 6 p 9.13]

45) What are reinsurance facilities (RF) and how do they operate? [EO 6 p 9.13]

46) Which state operates a state fund and how does it handle the residual market business? [EO 6 p 9.13]

47) Describe the purpose of AIPSO and its role in the automobile residual market. [EO 6 p 9.13]

48) List the roles AIPSO plays in the automobile residual market as an advisory organization. [EO 6 p 9.13-9.14]

49) List other ways in which AIPSO supports the residual market. [EO 6 p 9.13-9.14]

50) How does AIPSO support the distribution of business in the residual market? [EO 6 p 9.14]

51) Describe the purpose of the Commonwealth Automobile Reinsurers (CAR). [EO 7 p 9.14]

52) How does the Commonwealth Automobile Reinsurers operate? [EO 7 p 9.14]

53) What other functions does the Commonwealth Automobile Reinsurers perform? [EO 7 p 9.14]

54) Describe the purpose of the Independent Statistical Services (ISS) and provide a summary of their services. [EO 8 p 9.14-9.15]

55) What is Property Casualty Insurers Association of America (PCI) and what is its function? [EO 8 p 9.14]

56) What is the relationship between PCI and ISS? [EO 8 p 9.15]

57) What are ISS's primary products and services? [EO 8 p 9.15]

58) Provide examples of the techniques ISS uses to promote data quality. [EO 8 p 9.15]

59) Describe the purpose of ISO and provide a summary of its services. [EO 9 p 9.14-9.15]

60) List the services ISO provides to its members as a statistical agent. [EO 9 p 9.15]

61) List the services ISO provides to its members as an advisory organization. [EO 9 p 9.15]

62) What other information and services does ISO offer to members? [EO9 p 9.16]

63) Describe the purpose of the American Association of Insurance Services (AAIS) and provide a summary of their services. [EO 10 p 9.16]

64) What services does AAIS offer as a statistical agent? [EO 10 p 9.15]

65) What services does AAIS offer as an advisory organization? [EO 10 p 9.16]

66) Describe the purpose of the National Independent Statistical Service (NISS) and provide a brief summary of its services. [EO 11 p 9.16-9.17]

67) Describe the characteristics of data collection by NISS. [EO 11 p 9.16]

68) List the lines of insurance for which NISS publishes statistical plans. [EO 11 p 9.17]

69) What data quality services does NISS provide to its members? [EO 11 p 9.17]

70) Describe the purpose of the National Council on Compensation Insurance (NCCI) and provide a brief summary of its services. [EO 12 p 9.17-9.18]

71) List the NCCI's functions as a statistical agent and advisory agent. [EO 12 p 9.17]

72) How does the NCCI Data Manager Dashboard support reporting and data quality? [EO 12 p 9.17]

73) What types of data are collected by NCCI? [EO 12 p 9.17-9.18]

74) Briefly describe other workers' compensation data collection organizations. [EO 13 p 9.18]

75) What is the Workers Compensation Insurance Organization (WCIO)? [EO 13 p 9.18]

76) What is the purpose of the WCIO? [EO 13 p 9.18]

77) How did the WCIO facilitate information sharing between insurers and advisory organizations? [EO 13 p 9.18]

78) Describe the purpose of the International Association of Industrial Accident Boards and Commissions (IAIABC) and provide a summary of its services. [EO 14 p 9.18-9.19]

79) How does IAIABC's Electronic Data Interchange (EDI) Project facilitate data exchange? [EO 14 p 9.18]

80) Does IAIABC collect data as well as maintaining data standards? [EO 14 p 9.18]

81) Describe the purpose of the Surety & Fidelity Association of America (SFAA). [EO 15 p 9.19]

82) What is the difference between a fidelity bond and a surety bond? [EO 15 p 9.19]

83) What is the Surety & Fidelity Association of America (SFAA)? [EO 15 p 9.19]

84) What services does the SFAA offer its members? [EO 15 p 9.19]

Answers to Assignment 9 Questions

NOTE: These answers are provided to give students a basic understanding of acceptable types of responses. They are often not the only valid answers and are not intended to provide an exhaustive response to the questions.

Key Terms and Concepts

AIPSO: AIPSO, formerly called the Automobile Insurance Plans Service Organization, is an entity that provides a wide variety of services to residual markets in 49 states and the District of Columbia.

American Association of Insurance Services (AAIS): The American Association of Insurance Services (AAIS) acts as both a statistical agent and an advisory organization.

Assigned Risk Plans: Assigned risk plans, also called the residual market, are a source of coverage for insurance applicants who have been denied coverage by insurers writing policies in that jurisdiction.

Automobile insurance plans (AIP): In an AIP, private passenger residual market risks are distributed among, or assigned to, voluntary insurers based on the insurers' market share.

Calls for experience: Reporting instructions to insurers issued periodically by statistical agents.

Commercial automobile insurance plan (CAIP): A limited number of insurers act as servicing carriers for commercial residual market business.

Commonwealth Automobile Reinsurers (CAR): In Massachusetts, the Commonwealth Automobile Reinsurers (CAR) plan provides for liability and physical damage coverage for both private passenger and commercial vehicle operators who are unable to obtain coverage through the voluntary market.

Compensation Insurance Rating Board (CRIB): In New York, the Compensation Insurance Rating Board (CRIB) aggregates carriers' premium, loss, and payroll data to develop appropriate workers' compensation rate structures.

Data collection organizations (DCO): An agency that compiles statistical data, verifies the data's quality, reasonableness and completeness, and produces the required reports is a data collection organization.

Delaware Compensation Rating Bureau (DCRB): The licensed rating organization for workers' compensation services in Delaware.

Fidelity bond: Provides indemnification to the insured against losses resulting from dishonest or fraudulent acts committed by covered employees.

Independent Statistical Service (ISS): The Independent Statistical Service (ISS) is an approved statistical agent in 49 states, Puerto Rico, and the District of Columbia.

Insurance Services Office (ISO): Insurance Services Office (ISO) operates as an insurer advisory organization and is an authorized property and casualty statistical agent in all 50 states, the District of Columbia, and Puerto Rico, and it maintains the largest statistical database in the industry.

International Association of Industrial Accident Boards and Commissions (IAIABC): A nonprofit trade association whose membership includes agencies charged with the administration and regulation of workers' compensation; workers' compensation professionals, insurers, medical providers, law firms, and organizations involved in the electronic exchange of workers' compensation.

Joint underwriting associations (JUA): Nonprofit insurance pools established by a state legislature to establish servicing carriers for the residual market business for a particular line of insurance.

National Council on Compensation Insurance (NCCI): A statistical agent and advisory organization that focuses on workers' compensation insurance.

National Independent Statistical Service (NISS): An authorized statistical agent in all states except Texas, as well as in Washington D.C., and Puerto Rico.

New Jersey Compensation Rating and Inspection Bureau (NJCRIB): Administers workers' compensation rates and rating systems, classification systems, and the workers' compensation residual market.

Obligee: A party to which a principal has an obligation to perform is an obligee. In a surety contract, the obligee is the recipient of the performance from the principal, failing which, the surety offers financial compensation.

Pennsylvania Compensation Rating Bureau (PCRB): The licensed rating organization for workers' compensation in Pennsylvania.

Principal: In a surety contract, a company that has an obligation to perform to an obligee is referred to as a principal.

Reinsurance facilities (RF): Voluntary insurers in North Carolina and New Hampshire that write and service all applicants for coverage in a residual market, and the profit or loss is shared among the voluntary insurers in those jurisdictions.

Servicing carriers: When insurers are assigned policies under the assigned risk plan, in some jurisdictions, insurers have the option of paying a "buy-out fee" to transfer the responsibility for servicing assigned risks to other insurers within the AIP, referred to as servicing carriers.
Special calls: Calls to report data other than those included in the statistical plans and standard statistical reports.

Surety: A company that guarantees the performance of another company is called the surety (the principal).

Surety & Fidelity Association of America (SFAA): A national statistical reporting, ratemaking, and advisory organization for the surety and fidelity industry.

Surety bond: The agreement under which the surety agrees to compensate the obligee if the principal fails to perform.

Suretyship: A specialized type of insurance coverage in which one party guarantees the performance of a second party and offers financial compensation to a third party if the second party fails to meet their obligation.

State fund: A jurisdiction may establish a nonprofit called the state fund to handle residual market business.

Workers Compensation Insurance Organizations (WCIO): A voluntary association of statutorily authorized or licensed rating, advisory, or data service organizations that collect workers' compensation insurance information in one or more states.

Workers Compensation Rating and Inspection Bureau of Massachusetts (WCRIBMA): The state's licensed rating bureau.

Review Questions

1. **Explain the relationship between regulators and data collection organizations. [EO 1 p 9.7]**

Regulators need data from insurers and analytics to monitor market structure and performance. They sometimes lack the resources or expertise necessary for this function. Data collection organizations facilitate the exchange of data and intelligence between insurers and regulators.

2. **Explain the roles of statistical agents and advisory organizations. [EO 2 p 9.7]**

Statistical agents collect data from insurers as directed by regulators and provide aggregated reports in the predetermined format, as outlined in the statistical plan. Advisory organizations provide additional services, including developing loss costs, coverage and policy forms, researching the causes of loss and promoting loss prevention, advising on the impact of statutory changes, preparing manuals for rating rules, forms, and endorsements, and developing rating factors for rating variables.

3. **Why do advisory organizations develop loss costs rather than rates? [EO 2 p 9.7-9.8]**

There has been a move away from rate development, and at present, advisory organizations typically provide only loss-cost information to their member insurers. This helps preclude any potential appearance of collusion or price fixing.

4. **What are the data-related differences between a statistical agent and an advisory agent? [EO 2 p9.7-9.8]**

Statistical agents produce aggregate reports for regulators based on the requirements outlined in the NAIC Statistical Handbook, which specifies the content and format of those reports. To fulfill their mandate, advisory organizations require more detailed, comprehensive insurer data than statistical agents do.

5. **Why are advisory organizations advisory in nature? [EO 2, p9.8]**

These organizations are referred to as "advisory" because insurers are not obliged to use their rates and forms but may do so if they choose.

6. **What are some additional services an advisory organization might offer? [EO 2 p 9.8]**

- Researching the causes of losses and promoting loss prevention.
- Determining the impact of statutory changes.
- Preparing rating rules and manuals.
- Developing factors or formulas related to rating variables.
- Creating insurance policy forms and endorsements.

7. **What important roles do advisory organizations play for insurers, beyond regulatory reporting? [EO 2 p9.8]**

Advisory organizations are important to insurers because they provide aggregate industry data. An individual insurer may not have sufficient loss data to be able to make accurate actuarial projections for a particular line of business, type of policy, or territory. Access to aggregate data helps resolve this data shortfall.

8. **What is the importance of data standards to the data collection and reporting process? [EO 2 p 9.8]**

Data standards are an essential part of the data reporting and aggregating process. They facilitate the flow of data between organizations and help ensure that the data are valid and consistent.

9.   Explain the role statistical agents play in insurance regulation. [EO 3 p 9.8]

Statistical agents facilitate the data that regulators need to make important decisions about strategy and market environments and help regulators make the business of insurance efficient in their jurisdiction.

10.   List the lines of insurance for which statistical agents collect data. [EO 3 p 9.8-9.9]

- General liability (includes products liability and professional liability).
- Private passenger automobile.
- Commercial automobile.
- Homeowners and mobile homes.
- Dwelling fire and allied lines.
- Commercial/farm fire and allied lines.
- Inland marine.
- Business owners.
- Burglary and theft.
- Glass.
- Farmowners.
- Boiler and machinery.
- Medical professional liability.
- Comprehensive personal liability.
- Aircraft.
- Crop.
- Fidelity and surety.
- Mortgage guaranty.
- Workers' compensation.

11.   How does the use of statistical agents result in efficiencies for both regulators and insurers? [EO 3 p 9.9]

The use of statistical agents results in efficiencies for states and insurers by establishing centralized data collection systems.

12.   What are the advantages of a centralized data collection system? [EO 3 p 9.9]

A centralized data collection system avoids maintaining different systems for different states. It allows for uniform minimum reporting specifications, and a single set of reporting deadlines. It requires less record-keeping by providing a single set of updates to existing statistical plans and software edits.

13. Statistical agents provide what other service to the government at both the state and federal level? [EO 3 p 9.9]

Statistical agencies can also assist the government at both the state and federal levels in developing and implementing proposed data collection initiatives.

14. What are some of the activities a statistical agent performs to ensure regulators receive high-quality compilations? [EO 3 p 9.9]

Statistical agencies employ techniques to evaluate the quality and completeness of data to ensure regulators receive valid and complete statistical information. They combine the experience of all reporting companies and provide the state with aggregated reports. Statistical agents are also responsible for maintaining systems that reflect any change to the standard programs, classifications, or rating structures on file in a particular state. In addition to aggregating data at the state level, statistical agents can also provide data compilations on broader bases, for example countrywide, for comparison with a state's experience.

15. Why do statistical agents provide calls for experience to the insurers reporting to them? [EO 3 p 9.9]

While companies may use any method for recording statistics, including any format and coding structure convenient to their internal procedures, they must submit their experience to the statistical agent using the uniform codes and formats specified in the statistical plans. These calls for experience explain in detail when and how insurers must file their data.

16. What information does a call for experience include? [EO 3 p 9.9]

Calls for experience identify what information the companies must provide, for example the data elements and amount fields; when insurers must provide the data; and what data aggregation method they must use whether that be calendar-year, accident-year, or policy-year.

17. In general, how often do statistical agents issue calls for experience? [EO 9 p 9.9]

Statistical agents usually issue calls for experience annually, providing sufficient lead time to allow insurers to meet the specified filing date.

18. **What role do the statistical agent professional data managers, including statisticians and data processing analysts, play in the data collection process? {EO 3, p9.9]**

To ensure data quality and statistical accuracy, statistical agents employ statisticians, data processing analysts, and other professionals who use a variety of techniques to evaluate the quality, completeness, and reasonableness of the insurers' data. These checks help verify that insurers did not make systematic errors during production of their data files.

19. **Explain the reasons why state regulators issue calls for data and how these data are used. [EO 4 p 9.10]**

Regulators receive data from insurers according to the statistical plans on an ongoing basis, but sometimes they need additional or specific type of data to answer a particular question or resolve an issue/allegation. If the statistical agents do not have the data, then the regulator issues special calls for data. Regulators use this data to investigate allegations about market conduct or set strategy for the jurisdiction.

20. **Provide examples of situations where regulators might need additional data. [EO 4 p 9.10]**

Regulators may want to investigate allegations that insurers are refusing to provide coverage in particular geographic areas, a practice known as redlining, or understand the impact of a catastrophe on overall statewide results.

21. **What role can a statistical agent play to limit the regulators' need for a special call to insurers? [EO 9 p 9.10]**

Often, statistical agents can meet these needs directly by creating a customized report. Because they maintain a large base of insurers' statistical data, they can frequently provide the exact information requested, or information that is sufficiently similar, to meet the regulators' or the NAIC's requirements.

22. **How does the NAIC Statistical Handbook facilitate special calls? [EO 4 p 9.10]**

The NAIC Statistical Handbook includes a chapter containing guidelines and suggestions for reducing costs, and increasing uniformity, efficiencies and quality in the special call process.

23. **How does the NAIC facilitate special calls? [EO 4 p 9.10]**

NAIC maintains a website as a resource and a vehicle for improving regulators' communication with insurers during a special call.

24. What are some of the challenges special calls create for insurance data managers? [EO 4 p 9.10]

Special calls can create particular challenges for insurance data managers. For example, special calls may come at a time of year when data managers are already busy with financial reporting or regularly scheduled statistical reporting. The required data may not be adequately defined, and it may be unclear exactly what regulators need. Some data, such as incurred losses and incurred but not reported (IBNR) losses, are estimates and may not be available at a detailed class or coverage level. Timeframes may be relatively short.

25. What are some other sources for information that can be used to support a regulator's need for data? [EO 4 p 9.10]

Sometimes data that regulators want to examine may be found in an insurer's Annual Statement or may be available from an outside source.

26. What is the goal of insurance data managers with respect to special calls? [EO 4 p 9.10]

One important goal is to find a way to meet regulators' needs for data as efficiently and cost-effectively as possible.

27. Why do insurance data managers work closely with regulators when responding to a data call without any assistance from a DCO? [EO 4 p 9.10]

Data management professionals must understand when data must be collected and reported without help from a statistical agent or data collection organization. Working closely with regulators is critical in these situations. For example, a special call may request data that the insurer does not collect or would have great difficulty in collecting. Frequently, regulators may require fifteen to twenty years of historical data at a level of detail not captured in the statistical plan; this is especially the case in medical malpractice and liability claim special data calls.

28. Why is accuracy important for data reported in a special call? [EO 4 p 9.10]

Regulators use the data to determine whether changes to rates and/or loss costs are necessary. Often, special calls are commissioned by the state legislature or the state DOI to determine if new or revised legislation is required for insurance coverage, especially in emerging markets. The insurer is frequently required to attest, via affidavit, to the accuracy of the data provided in response to the data call.

29.

30. Describe how data management at a data collection organization differs from that at an insurance company. [EO 5 p 9.11]

Data management at insurers and DCOs is comparable from various perspectives yet varies in different ways. Data at an insurance company is verifiable from the source, which a DCO cannot do due to lack of access to the source of data. DCOs depend on data accuracy through reasonableness and completeness techniques. Insurers must use data quality tools to derive data from unstructured sources such as pictures and claim reports or adjuster's notes. DCOs receive data in accordance with the statistical plan, so they do not have to deal with this type of complexity. Insurers may collect detailed data for internal use and map from their source for statistical reporting. Sometimes, there is discrepancy in this mapping, so DCOs do not receive the intended data. Insurers need their data well integrated between their various departments/functions, such as underwriting, billing, claims etc. DCOs have fewer systems integration needs.

31. What is the difference between insurers and DCOs with respect to confirming the accuracy of data? [EO 5 p 9.11]

Insurers have access to source documents if there is a need to verify the data they use internally. If a question arises about particular data, the insurer's data management team can request confirmation from underwriting, policy issuance, or claims about the data in question. DCOs generally do not have access to this material and can only infer the quality of the data using reasonableness and completeness techniques. In some instances, the DCO manager may request a check of the source records by the insurer.

32. What is the difference between insurers and DCOs with respect to the structure of data? [EO 5 p 9.11]

DCOs typically request and collect data in highly structured record formats. Insurers have significant amounts of data in non-standard formats, including photographs, claim reports, and adjuster's notes. As a result, insurance company data managers require data quality tools and storage options that DCO data managers may not need.

33. What challenges do insurers and DCOs face regarding the codes and information collected from insurers? [EO 5 p 9.11]

Insurers may use additional, expanded codes and information internally to capture greater detail about their business than is defined in their DCO's statistical plan. In this case, when reporting to a DCO, they need to map the data in their internal records to the DCO's statistical data requirements. This poses a challenge for both the insurer and the DCO. From the insurer's perspective, it is important that the mapping ensures that high-quality, meaningful data are reported to the DCO. The DCO data manager needs to understand that the data received may be mapped and that mapping may not necessarily represent what is expected.

34. Why is system integration usually more involved for insurers than for DCO's? [EO 5 p 9.11]

Insurance companies need high-quality, consistent data to flow through several key systems: policy issuance, billing, claims, ratemaking, management reporting, and statistical reporting. The challenges of meeting this requirement are complex. DCOs may have fewer systems using reported data that need to be integrated, for example, data collection systems, edit systems, regulatory reporting, and perhaps, ratemaking systems.

35. Why might insurer and DCO systems be incompatible? [EO 5 p 9.11]

As a result of mappings, systems integration, and system update priorities, internal company data and statistical data may seem incompatible. An insurer's premium and loss systems may be updated at different times since the changes are needed in the premium system long before they may be needed in the loss system. Additionally, statistical systems may be the last to be updated due to valid company priorities. As DCO data managers review and question statistical data, the challenge for company data managers is tracking all the data manipulation in their systems to resolve anomalies. This may be complicated by the time lag between when statistical data are reported and when the DCO data manager identifies and questions reported data.

36. Statistical agents require insurers to reconcile statistical data to the insurer's Annual Statement. What is the challenge for both insurer and DCO? [EO 5 p 9.12]

The challenge here for both DCO and insurer data managers is reconciling statistical and financial data which by their very nature are not necessarily directly comparable.

37. While security is a key concern for both insurers and DCOs, what is the difference in focus? [EO 5 p 9.12]

Insurer data managers must keep data secure through a number of systems and databases. Their responsibility is to their policyholders and claimants. A key DCO security concern is to protect individual companies' trade secrets which might be lost in a data breech, but also revealed unwittingly in analyses and reports released by the DCO.

38. Describe the fundamental difference between insurer and DCO data management. [EO 5 p 9.12]

Insurers collect data at various points in their process and at different locations. They have considerable control over data collection processes and procedures. DCOs, on the other hand, collect data from hundreds of insurance companies, each with its own statistical reporting procedures. A major concern for DCO data managers is compiling meaningful reports and analyses from different insurers whose data may not be consistent with one another.

39. What is the purpose of the automobile residual market? [EO 6 p 9.12]

The purpose of a residual market is to make automobile liability coverage available to vehicle owners who are unable to obtain coverage in the standard, or voluntary, market, often because of a poor driving record.

40. In addition to automobile, what other lines of insurance have residual market coverage? [EO 6 p 9.12]

Residual market coverage is also available for commercial property and workers' compensation risks in some states.

41. List the approaches for providing automobile residual market coverage. [EO 6 p 9.12]

- Automobile insurance plans (AIP).
- Commercial automobile insurance plan (CAIP).
- Joint underwriting associations (JUA).
- Reinsurance facilities (RF).
- State funds.

42. How does an automobile insurance plan (AIP) work? [EO 6 p 9.12]

In an AIP, private passenger residual market risks are distributed among or assigned to voluntary insurers based on each insurer's market share. An insurer with a larger proportion of the voluntary automobile market would receive more residual market risks than an insurer writing a smaller proportion of the voluntary market. Insurers are able to charge appropriately higher rates for this assigned business; they service it as they do their standard insureds.

43. What is a servicing carrier in an automobile insurance plan? [EO 6 p 9.12]

In some jurisdictions, insurers have the option of paying a "buy-out fee" to transfer the responsibility for servicing assigned risks to other insurers within the AIP. These other insurers are referred to as servicing carriers.

44. How does a commercial automobile insurance plan (CAIP) work? [EO 6 p 9.13]

In a commercial automobile insurance plan (CAIP), a limited number of insurers act as servicing carriers for commercial residual market business. The servicing carriers essentially transfer the operating results associated with this business to the CAIP, which in turn apportions those results proportionally to all voluntary insurers licensed to write commercial automobile insurance within the jurisdiction based on their relative market share.

45. What is a joint underwriting association (JUA) and how does it operate? [EO 6 p 9.13]

Joint underwriting associations (JUA) are insurance pools. Typically, state law requires all insurers licensed to write automobile insurance in the state to participate in the pool. A subset of participants acts as servicing carriers and the operating results of the JUA are distributed to participants based on their share of the voluntary market.

46. What are reinsurance facilities (RF) and how do they operate? [EO 6 p 9.13]

In states with reinsurance facilities (RF), voluntary insurers write and service all applicants for coverage. Residual market risks are not assigned, and the amount of residual market business a particular insurer writes is not dependent on that carrier's voluntary market share. Underwriters are permitted to charge appropriately higher rates for residual market risks and may cede the associated premiums and losses to a state reinsurance facility. Profits or losses on reinsured policies are shared among the voluntary auto insurers within the jurisdiction.

47. Which state operates a state fund and how does it handle the residual market business? [EO 6 p 9.13]

The state of Maryland operates the Maryland Automobile Insurance Fund (MAIF) to handle residual market business. Insurance companies in the voluntary market do not participate directly in MAIF in terms of writing and servicing policies. However, they are required to subsidize any MAIF operating losses and may surcharge their own policyholders to recover any such subsidies.

48. Describe the purpose of AIPSO and its role in the automobile residual market. [EO 6 p 9.13]

Automobile insurance is mandatory, but some applicants cannot get coverage for a variety of reasons. When standard insurance companies decline coverage, AIPSO meets the needs of these applicants.

49. List the roles AIPSO plays in the automobile residual market as a advisory organization. [EO 6 p 9.13-9.14]

- The organization is licensed as a rating organization in more than 40 states and is authorized to collect data from statistical organizations and develop and file rates and rating rules with regulators.
- AIPSO develops insurance policies specifically for the residual market.
- AIPSO can conduct on-site audits of servicing carriers.

- It communicates with state regulators and acts as a liaison between regulators and residual market governing bodies.
- AIPSO supports residual market mechanisms in such areas as the analysis of insurance data and operating results; the development of uniform accounting and statistical rules; and the preparation of detailed management information reports.
- AIPSO develops and adjusts ratios for sharing residual market insurance applications among insurers and determines how operating results of the residual market are to be distributed among insurers.

50. List other ways in which AIPSO supports the residual market {EO 6 p 9.13-9.14]

- In a number of jurisdictions, AIPSO acts as plan manager for the residual market mechanism.
- It can offer legal services for residual market organizations.
- It also provides insurance application processing services, receiving applications from producers, assigning them to insurers or servicing carriers, binding coverage electronically, and answering customer service inquiries from insureds, producers, and carriers.
- The organization offers planning, design, support, and coordination services for residual market information systems.
- It supports and monitors the licensing of residual market producers.
- Professionals employed at AIPSO can offer management expertise and consulting services to residual market mechanisms for which AIPSO is not the plan manager.
- The organization supports vehicle safety by liaising with companies that perform safety inspections on commercial vehicles.
- It also works with a vendor to provide back-up underwriting, claims settlement, and customer relations services for commercial automobile insurance plan (CAIP) business.
- AIPSO offers accounting and investment services for residual market mechanisms, including processing accounts receivable and payable; maintaining accounting records; preparing financial statements and tax filings; and overseeing the organization's investments.
- AIPSO is also actively involved at both the state and federal levels in preventing insurance fraud in residual markets.

51. How does AIPSO support the distribution of business in the residual market? [EO 6 p 9.14]

Complying with the rules of each jurisdiction, AIPSO maintains a quota and risk-assignment system for the distribution of AIP business. The subscriber companies supply the basic data used for these calculations and formulas that determine how assignments are distributed. AIPSO requires calendar-year data about the number of car years an insurer writes in the voluntary market. In some states, insurers are given credit for writing certain types of risks, for example, drivers under 26 or over 65, in the voluntary market and that credit needs to be factored into the calculation of the insurer's residual market quota. AIPSO also requires data about the insurer's current volume of residual market risks. Based on these data, AIPSO calculates the insurer's residual market quota and assigns risks based on that quota.

52. Describe the purpose of the Commonwealth Automobile Reinsurers (CAR). [EO 7 p 9.14]

In Massachusetts, the Commonwealth Automobile Reinsurers (CAR) plan provides for liability and physical damage coverage for both private passenger and commercial vehicle operators who are unable to obtain coverage through the voluntary market.

53. How does the Commonwealth Automobile Reinsurers operate? [EO 7 p 9.14]

All insurers licensed to write private passenger coverage in Massachusetts are required to become members of CAR and to accept assignments through the Massachusetts Auto Insurance Plan (MAIP). Licensed writers of commercial motor vehicle coverage participate in the financial results of the residual market pool, and some function as servicing carriers.

54. What other functions does the Commonwealth Automobile Reinsurers perform? [EO 7 p 9.14]

In addition, CAR operates as a statistical agent in Massachusetts for private passenger and commercial automobile coverages, collecting, editing, and processing premium and loss statistics. The organization publishes a commercial statistical plan, a private passenger statistical plan, and documents on annual statement reconciliation, statistical edits, and lookups. It also offers support to members in such areas as administrative procedures, performance standards, experience rating, and telecommunications.

55. Describe the purpose of the Independent Statistical Services (ISS) and provide a summary of their services. [EO 8 p 9.14-9.15]

ISS is a statistical agent and a subsidiary of PCI. This trade organization advocates on behalf of its member companies with state and federal regulators, and keeps members informed on key issues affecting the insurance industry. The primary products ISS produces are annual statistical compilations for regulators and subscribers. ISS also produces ratemaking support data and assists with special data calls. ISS Fast Track Plus facilitates claims trend analysis, and ISS assists subscribers by reviewing their books of business and informational assistance through training and newsletters.

56. What is Property Casualty Insurers Association of America (PCI) and what is its function? [EO 8 p 9.14]

PCI is a trade organization that advocates on behalf of its member companies with state and federal regulators, and keeps members informed on key issues affecting the insurance industry.

57. What is the relationship between PCI and ISS? [EO 8 p 9.15]

ISS is a subsidiary of the Property Casualty Insurers Association of America (PCI).

58. What are ISS's primary products and services? [EO 8 p 9.15]

- ISS publishes statistical plans to help insurers code and report statistical data with common data definitions and formats.
- ISS produces annual statistical compilations that are filed with state regulators by line of business. These compilations meet the basic statistical reporting requirements, so insurers need not report data at the more detailed level required for ratemaking.
- ISS makes these data compilations available to subscribing insurers as well.
- In addition to these reports, ISS produces data to support ratemaking.
- ISS will also respond, on behalf of subscribers, to regulators' special calls in cases in which ISS has the required data.
- For insurers writing homeowners and private passenger automobile insurance, the ISS Fast Track Plus™ product facilitates claims trend analysis to support improved underwriting.

59. Provide examples of the techniques ISS uses to promote data quality. [EO 8 p 9.15]

- To help ensure compliance with regulatory reporting standards, ISS conducts periodic reviews of subscribers' books of business to compare them with their statistical reporting.
- ISS also evaluates subscribers' submissions in terms of submission balancing, code editing, distributional comparisons, and financial reconciliation.
- Insurers can file statistics with ISS on the organization's website.
- ISS also offers statistical reporting training workshops as well as informal assistance to subscribing insurers.
- The ISS newsletter, Statistically Speaking, keeps subscribers informed on trends and emerging issues that could affect statistical reporting.

60. Describe the purpose of ISO and provide a summary of their services. [EO 9 p 9.14-9.15]

ISO operates as a statistical reporting agency and a source of data for fraud bureaus, fire marshals, etc., and an insurer advisory organization. ISO provides regulatory and compliance assistance through insurance forms, loss costs, and products such as the State Filing Handbook, the Commercial Lines Manual, and the Personal Lines Manual. ISO and its subsidiary, Verisk Analytics, provide services, programs, and support in a number of areas, including underwriting and rating, data and statistics, analytics, premium audit, market expansion, catastrophe management, compliance and reporting, data and statistical services, excess insurance, and reinsurance and surplus lines. In addition, ISO offers training, resources, and technical advisory services.

61. List the services ISO provides to its members as a statistical agent. [EO 9 p 9.15]

- ISO publishes commercial and personal lines statistical plans.
- ISO submits summaries of the information collected from members to insurance regulators.

- ISO also provides data on behalf of its member insurers to state fraud bureaus, fire marshals, and other groups.

62. List the services ISO provides to its members as an advisory organization. [EO 9 p 9.15]

- The information it collects is used to develop products and services that help insurers compete in the marketplace.
- ISO offers a variety of personal and commercial lines insurance programs.
- It also publishes a Commercial Lines Manual, which includes the rules, state exceptions, loss costs, and policy and endorsement forms for each ISO line of business and jurisdiction. It also publishes a Personal Lines Manual.
- It publishes a State Filing Handbook that includes information about state filing laws, regulations, and procedures.

63. What other information and services does ISO offer to members? [EO9 p 9.16]

ISO offers member insurers online access, via ISONet®, to a wide variety of information in the following areas:

- Underwriting and rating.
- Data and statistics.
- Claims.
- Analytics.
- Loss control.
- Workers' compensation.
- Regulatory compliance.
- Premium audit.

The organization provides services, programs, and support in a number of areas, including market expansion, catastrophe management, compliance and reporting, data and statistical services, excess insurance, and reinsurance and surplus lines. In addition, ISO offers training, resources, and technical advisory services.

64. Describe the purpose of the American Association of Insurance Services (AAIS) and provide a brief summary of their services. [EO 10 p 9.16]

AAIS acts as both a statistical agent and an advisory organization. AAIS maintains statistical plans for personal, commercial, and agricultural lines, maintains policy forms and endorsements, manual rules, and rating information, and provides members with the detailed data necessary for ratemaking. AAIS Statistical Data Management Application (SDMA) is an online application that facilitates online transaction statistical reporting.

65. What services does AAIS offer as a statistical agent? [EO 10 p 9.15]

- AAIS maintains statistical plans for personal, commercial, and agricultural lines, collecting data at the transaction level.
- AAIS accepts statistical reporting data in a variety of file formats, provides detailed documentation on the required data types, offers technical and analytical support for data extraction, and works with insurers to develop and implement a statistical reporting process.
- The AAIS Statistical Data Management Application (SDMA) is an online application that facilitates online transaction statistical reporting.

66. What services does AAIS offer as an advisory organization [EO 10 p 9.16]

In its advisory capacity, AAIS develops and maintains policy forms and endorsements, manual rules, and rating information for over 34 different programs in personal, commercial, agricultural, and inland marine lines of insurance. It maintains a cloud-based AAIS Underwriting Platform that allows members to underwrite and rate policies that are based on these AAIS programs.

The organization ensures that all its programs comply with all applicable legislation and regulations. AAIS actuarial services develop loss costs, rate indications, and rate relativities. It offers a Homeowners By-Peril Rating Plan that allows insurers to price each homeowners policy based on the specific risk characteristics it represents. AAIS has assembled vendors for underwriting, marketing, and loss control information, called the AAIS Alliance; members can access this information through the AAISdirect portal. AAISdirect is an online service that gives members access to all of the products and services AAIS offers.

67. Describe the purpose of the National Independent Statistical Service (NISS) and provide a brief summary of their services. [EO 11 p 9.16-9.17]

NISS is a statistical agent that assists insurers in reporting data for all lines except workers' compensation at the summary level and annually (unless prohibited by the jurisdiction), thereby promoting simplicity.

68. Describe the characteristics of data collection by NISS. [EO 11 p 9.16]

NISS statistical plans comply with the minimum reporting requirements outlined in the National Association of Insurance Commissioners (NAIC) Statistical Handbook and NISS members are required to report only summary data rather than transaction-level data. Their objective is to keep the statistical reporting process as simple as possible. Members report data annually except in jurisdictions that require quarterly reporting.

69. List the lines of insurance for which NISS publishes statistical plans. [EO 11 p 9.17]

- Personal and commercial liability, no-fault, and physical damage automobile coverage is written in the voluntary and assigned risk markets in most states.
- Commercial lines.
- Homeowners and allied lines.
- Other than auto, which is used for both personal and commercial insurance coverages such as burglary and theft, farmowners, fidelity, forgery and surety, general liability including professional liability, glass, inland marine, medical professional liability, and personal liability.

70. What data quality services does NISS provide it members? [EO 11 p 9.17]

NISS allows members to securely upload data files via the NISS website and check the status of their filings. The website also provides access to data quality reports, timeliness reports, call instructions, statistical plans, filing schedules, and information bulletins. NISS provides its members with tools that enable data managers to validate and edit data before submission. The organization also provides workshops and training videos, and information bulletins to educate members about the statistical reporting process.

71. Describe the purpose of the National Council on Compensation Insurance (NCCI) and provide a brief summary of their services. [EO 12 p 9.17-9.18]

NCCI is a statistical agent and advisory organization for the workers' compensation insurance market in all states except those that adopt independent or monopoly systems. Insurers are required to report a variety of data to NCCI including data on voluntary and assigned risk coverage; exposure, premium and loss information; aggregated premium, losses, expenses, and claim count data that indicate the company's overall performance; specific data about deaths and permanent total disabilities; data from medical bills; and premium, loss, and expense data related to participation in a residual market pool.

72. List the NCCI's functions as a statistical agent and advisory agent. [EO 12 p 9.17]

- Analyzes industry trends.
- Prepares workers' compensation insurance rate recommendations.
- Assists in pricing proposed legislation.
- Provides a variety of data products to maintain a healthy workers' compensation system and reduce the frequency of employee injuries.
- Offers a wide variety of publications, reports, resources, and tools related to data reporting, general industry information, residual markets, and underwriting.
- Provides support for agents and brokers and maintains a learning center.

73. How does the NCCI Data Manager Dashboard support reporting and data quality? [EO 12 p 9.17]

The NCCI Data Manager Dashboard allows data managers to monitor data reporting performance, compare year-over-year trends and their impact, and view detailed and summary results.

74. What types of data are collected by NCCI? [EO 12 p 9.17-9.18]

Insurers are required to report a variety of data to NCCI including data on voluntary and assigned risk coverage; exposure, premium and loss information; aggregated premium, losses, expenses, and claim count data that indicate the company's overall performance; specific data about deaths and permanent total disabilities; data from medical bills; and premium, loss, and expense data related to participation in a residual market pool.

75. Briefly describe other workers' compensation data collection organizations. [EO 13 p 9.18]

- **California**: The WCIRB provides workers' compensation advisory premiums as well as research, information, and educational services.
- **New York**: The Compensation Insurance Rating Board (CRIB) aggregates carriers' premium, loss, and payroll data to develop appropriate workers' compensation rate structures.
- **New Jersey**: Compensation Rating and Inspection Bureau (NJCRIB) administers workers' compensation rates and rating systems, classification systems, and the workers' compensation residual market.
- **Massachusetts**: The Workers Compensation Rating and Inspection Bureau of Massachusetts (WCRIBMA) is the licensed rating bureau.
- **Pennsylvania**: The Pennsylvania Compensation Rating Bureau (PCRB) is the licensed rating organization for workers' compensation.
- **Delaware**: The Delaware Compensation Rating Bureau (DCRB) provides similar services.

76. What is the Workers Compensation Insurance Organization (WCIO)? [EO 13 p 9.18]

The WCIO is a voluntary association of statutorily authorized or licensed rating, advisory, or data service organizations that collect workers compensation insurance information and provide a forum for the exchange of information about workers compensation insurance.

77. What is the purpose of the WCIO? [EO 13 p 9.18]

The purpose of the WCIO is to provide a forum for exchanging information about workers' compensation insurance.

78. How did the WCIO facilitate information sharing between insurers and advisory organizations? [EO 13 p 9.18]

The WCIO has developed standards for the electronic transmission of information between insurers and rating/advisory organizations. These specifications are available for policy information, unit statistical reporting, experience modifications, detailed claim information, and individual case reports."

79. Describe the purpose of the International Association of Industrial Accident Boards and Commissions (IAIABC) and provide a summary of its services. [EO 14 p 9.18-9.19]

IAIABC is a nonprofit trade association with membership including agencies charged with the administration and regulation of WC; WC professionals, insurers, medical providers, law firms, and organizations involved in the electronic exchange of WC data. IAIABC is an intermediary between jurisdictions and insurers in data reporting matters.

80. How does IAIABC's Electronic Data Interchange (EDI) Project facilitate data exchange? [EO 14 p 9.18]

The IAIABC's Electronic Data Interchange (EDI) Project develops and maintains standards for electronic exchange and reporting of workers' compensation data.

81. Does IAIABC collect data as well as maintain data standards? [EO 14 p 9.18]

From an insurer perspective, the IAIABC operates similarly to a DCO in that it collects data from the individual insurers.

82. Describe the purpose of the Surety & Fidelity Association of America (SFAA). [EO 15 p 9.19]

SFAA is a national statistical reporting, ratemaking, and advisory organization for the surety and fidelity industry. It fulfills its role in an advisory capacity by developing rules, procedures, risk classification systems, and loss costs, using ACORD standards for data communication, and serves as a clearinghouse for surety information.

83. What is the difference between a fidelity bond and a surety bond? [EO 15 p 9.19]

A fidelity bond provides indemnification protection for the insured against losses resulting from dishonest and fraudulent acts committed by covered employees. Covered acts include such things as theft, forgery, robbery, and safe burglary. A surety **bond** is the agreement under which the surety (the party guaranteeing performance) agrees to compensate the obligee (the party receiving the benefit of that performance) if the principal (the party that has the obligation to perform) fails to perform.

84. What is the Surety & Fidelity Association of America (SFAA)? [EO 15 p 9.19]

The Surety & Fidelity Association of America (SFAA) is a national statistical reporting, ratemaking, and advisory organization for the surety and fidelity industry.

85. What services does the SFAA offer its members? [EO 15 p 9.19]

- As a statistical agent in all jurisdictions other than Texas, SFAA publishes statistical plans and information on data reporting.
- In an advisory capacity, SFAA develops rules, procedures, risk classification systems, and loss costs.
- SFAA supports the use of ACORD standards for data communication and the standardization of bond form numbers, and serves as a clearinghouse for information on automation and best practices.
- SFAA offers members information about trends, developments, and technologies; provides education; and offers additional services.
- The organization is active in advocacy at both the state and federal levels.

Data Management at a
Property and Casualty Statistical Agent

Educational Objectives

Upon completion of this assignment, you should be able to:

1. Describe the different methods of data collection used by statistical agents.
2. Describe the pros and cons of each data collection method.
3. Identify common data quality issues with each collection method.
4. Explain how the data collection performed by statistical agents relates to the requirements of the NAIC Handbook.
5. For each data collection method, describe the data quality efforts statistical agents use to confirm the reasonableness of the data reported to them.
6. For most lines of insurance, the NAIC Handbook requires multiple years of experience. Explain how the data collection method addresses the maturing of loss and premium data over time.
7. Identify the major property and casualty statistical agents and the lines of insurance data collected by each.
8. For each data collection method, describe the data quality efforts statistical agents use to confirm the completeness of the data reported to them.
9. For each data collection method, describe the data quality efforts statistical agents use to confirm the validity of the data reported to them.
10. Identify how stat agents use the data collected for uses beyond regulatory reporting.

For each assignment, define or describe each of the Key Terms and Concepts and answer each of the Review and Discussion Questions.

Key Terms and Concepts

Absolute Accuracy:

Accelerated Reports:

Accident Year:

Annual Statistical Compilations:

Calendar Year:

Collected Earned Premiums:

Content Edit:

Distributional Edits:

Effective accuracy:

Fast Track Monitoring System:

Field Edit:

Field Relationship Edits:

Incurred but Not Reported (IBNR):

Monopolistic state funds:

Policy Year:

Reasonableness:

Relational Edit:

Relative accuracy:

Special Statistical Call:

Statistical Agent:

Statistical Call:

Statistical Plan:

Transaction based statistical plans:

Unit Statistical Report:

Review Questions

1. Describe the different methods of data collection used by statistical agents.

2. Describe the pros and cons of each data collection method.

3. Identify common data quality issues with each collection method.

4. Explain how the data collection performed by statistical agents relates to the requirements of the NAIC Handbook.

5. For each data collection method, describe the data quality efforts statistical agents use to confirm the reasonableness of the data reported to them.

6. For most lines of insurance, the NAIC Handbook requires multiple years of experience. Explain how the data collection method addresses the maturing of loss and premium data over time.

7. For each data collection method, describe the data quality efforts statistical agents use to confirm the completeness of the data reported to them.

8. For each data collection method, describe the data quality efforts statistical agents use to confirm the validity of the data reported to them.

9. Identify how stat agents use the data collected for uses beyond regulatory reporting.

Answers to Assignment 10 Questions

NOTE: These answers are provided to give students a basic understanding of acceptable types of responses. They are often not the only valid answers and are not intended to provide an exhaustive response to the questions.

Key Terms and Concepts

Absolute Accuracy: Means that the data is 100 percent correct. It contains no known errors.

Accelerated Reports: Accelerated reports contain premium and loss information by state for each accounting quarter.

Accident Year: Accident year experience shows the premiums earned and losses incurred during a 12-month period.

Annual Statistical Compilations: Detailed annual reports that are used to evaluate the historic experience of specific lines of insurance.

Calendar Year: The premiums earned during a 12-month period and losses incurred during a 12-month period, regardless of the effective dates of the policy on which those transactions occurred.

Collected Earned Premiums: The portion of written premiums actually collected by the insurer during the period covered in the report.

Content Edit: The content edit checks reported data to see if a reported code is defined in accordance with the statistical plan.

Distributional Edits: Checks performed by a statistical agent that compare submitted data with historical profiles for specific data elements, such as state, territory, class, and coverage, for the company and the industry to identify systematic errors.

Effective accuracy: Means there are some imperfections in the data, but the data is generally usable.

Fast Track Monitoring System: Fast Track Monitoring System uses quarterly premium and loss data to aggregate data by state only for the major lines of coverage.

Field Edit: The checks performed on data to verify that the proper type of information is coded in each field, conforming to the Statistical Plan.

Field Relationship Edits: Checks performed on data for the relationships among codes in two or more fields on the detail record.

Incurred but Not Reported (IBNR): A term in reference to losses to identify a loss that occurred within a time frame but will not be reported to an insurer until a future specified date.

Monopolistic state funds: Monopolistic state funds have state-controlled workers' compensation plans that prohibit private insurers from competitively writing this coverage.

Policy Year: The premium and loss transaction on policies effective during a specific 12-month period.

Reasonableness: The data is consistent with prior data, previous company submissions, known changes in that line of business, and industry trends.

Relational Edit: A relational edit verifies that a code reported by the insurer is valid in combination with one or more related fields.

Relative accuracy: Relative accuracy of data is when data is coded inaccurately as to its definition but reported consistently over time.

Special Statistical Call: A Special Statistical Call is a call for data by statistical agent. The call may be for information about a specific line of insurance in a specific state, as required by the state or the NAIC.

Statistical Agent: An organization created to gather data, analyze it, and provide statistical reporting services to the insurance industry.

Statistical Call: Calls for data issued by statistical agents to insurance companies to inform them about the nature of data requested, the due dates, and the technical requirements.

Statistical Plan: A plan devised by a statistical agent, filed with the regulator to collect data.

Transaction-based statistical plans: Collect very detailed information at the transaction level and are usually collected quarterly, though they may also be collected monthly.

Unit Statistical Report: The data required to be submitted for all NCCI states covered on each policy, providing audited exposure, premium, and loss information for that policy.

Review Questions

1. Describe the different methods of data collection used by statistical agents.

Statistical agents collect financial and statistical data to provide information on premium and loss experience, solvency, market trends, and the relationship between rates and coverages. Statistical agents collect this data by devising the statistical plan to obtain this data from insurers or by issuing special statistical calls.

2. Describe the pros and cons of each data collection method.

Comprehensive reports may be costly, as insurers need greater investment in technology and human expertise to cover all data points; at the same time, abbreviated reports may not provide the regulator with all the data they need to analyze the market and set strategy. Aggregated reports are efficient but may not provide the granularity of detail required as well as become difficult to identify inaccuracies.

3. Identify common data quality issues with each collection method.

Data quality concerns emanate from issues about validity, accuracy, completeness, and reasonableness.

4. Explain how the data collection performed by statistical agents relates to the requirements of the NAIC Handbook.

The NAIC Handbook outlines the scope and data requirements of NAIC in 3 basic report designs: Annual Statistical Compilations, Fast Track Monitoring System, and Accelerated reports. Statistical Agents collect data in accordance with the NAIC Handbook.

5. For each data collection method, describe the data quality efforts statistical agents use to confirm the reasonableness of the data reported to them.

Statistical agents ensure high standards of data quality by checking the validity, accuracy, completeness, and reasonableness of the data.

6. For most lines of insurance, the NAIC Handbook requires multiple years of experience. Explain how the data collection method addresses the maturing of loss and premium data over time.

When regulators and the NAIC need a 5-10 year history to see the development of trends in premium, loss, and reserving strategies, statistical agents account for inflation, deductibles, retention, and policy limits in evaluating data. They also allow the exclusion of IBNR for reporting, exclude the factored amount, and extend the loss valuation timing.

7. **For each data collection method, describe the data quality efforts statistical agents use to confirm the completeness of the data reported to them.**

Analysis of company data includes balancing and reconciliation procedures, editing for invalid codes, and checking the distribution of data among the various data elements. The reported premiums and paid losses are matched against the company's "Statutory Page 14" of the annual statement, comparing the statistical records to the company's financial records.

8. **For each data collection method, describe the data quality efforts statistical agents use to confirm the validity of the data reported to them.**

Statistical agents confirm the validity of data reported to them through extensive, comprehensive edit checks. They may be through Field Edits, Field Relationship Edits, Distributional Edits, Report Edits and Content Edits.

9. **Identify how stat agents use the data collected for uses beyond regulatory reporting.**

Data collected for statistical reporting may also be used for:

- Compliance.
- Actuarial Purposes Such As Loss Cost Development And Ratemaking.
- Residual Market Analysis.
- Trend Data Experience.
- Monitor The Performance Of Companies In The Market.
- Semiannual Reports Of Summarized Premium And Loss Information.
- Advisory Services.
- Economic Research.
- Statistical Modeling.

Data Management at a State Insurance Regulatory Agency

Educational Objectives

Upon completion of this assignment, you should be able to:

1. Explain the relationship between regulators and data collection organizations.
2. Describe the role that each of the following has in state insurance regulation:
   a. Licensing.
   b. Ensuring Clarity and Consistency.
   c. Protecting Insurance Consumers.
   d. Facilitating Affordable and Available Coverage.
   e. Maintaining Financial Solvency of Insurance Companies.
3. Explain the different types of rate, rule, and policy from regulatory laws.
4. Explain the difference between financial data and statistical data.
5. Outline the objective, features, and benefits of the Statistical Data Monitoring System (SDMS).
6. Explain the reasons for a special call.
7. Explain insurance regulators' concerns about data quality and possible solutions to those concerns.
8. Distinguish the regulation of workers' compensation insurance from other lines of insurance.
9. Explain how each of the following informs insurance regulators:
   a. National Association of Insurance Commissioners.
   b. International Association of Industrial Accident Boards and Commissions.
   c. National Council on Compensation Insurance.
   d. Other insurance-related organizations.

For each assignment, define or describe each of the Key Terms and Concepts and answer each of the Review and Discussion Questions.

Key Terms and Concepts

Advisory organization:

Advisory Organization Examination Oversight Working Group:

Antifraud Technology Working Group:

Audit Trail:

Auto Insurance Working Group:

Big Data Working Group:

Data Dictionary:

File and Use Laws:

Financial data:

Market Conduct Examination:

No File:

Prior Approval Law:

Rating Bureau:

Risk-Based Capital:

Special calls:

Statistical Agents:

Statistical Data:

Statistical Data Monitoring System:

Statistical Data Working Group:

Trade associations:

Use and File:

Review Questions

1. Describe the role of licensing in state insurance regulation.

2. How do regulators ensure clarity and consistency among insurers?

3. What are some ways that regulators protect insurance consumers?

4. How do regulators facilitate affordable and available coverage?

5. What are some methods available to regulators to maintain financial solvency of insurance companies?

6. Explain the difference between financial data and statistical data.

7. Outline the objective, features and benefits of the Statistical Data Monitoring System (SDMS).

8. Explain the reasons for a special call.

9. Explain insurance regulators' concerns about data quality and possible solutions to those concerns.

10. Distinguish the regulation of workers' compensation insurance from other lines of insurance.

11. What is the role of the International Association of Industrial Accident Boards and Commissions (IAIABC)?

12. How does National Council on Compensation Insurance (NCCI) influence the workers' compensation market?

Answers to Assignment 11 Questions

NOTE: These answers are provided to give students a basic understanding of acceptable types of responses. They are often not the only valid answers and are not intended to provide an exhaustive response to the questions.

Key Terms and Concepts

Advisory organization: An organization licensed by state insurance regulators to make rate or loss cost filings, collect loss and expense statistical data and make recommendations to insurers and regulators.

Advisory Organization Examination Oversight Working Group: A working group within the Property and Casualty Insurance Committee at NAIC to monitor the data reporting and data-collection processes of advisory organizations, rating organizations, and statistical agents to ensure data quality.

Antifraud Technology Working Group: A subgroup within the Antifraud Task Force under the Market Regulation and Consumer Affairs Committee called the Antifraud Technology Working Group to evaluate sources of antifraud data and help develop ways to enhance data exchange among regulators, fraud investigators, law enforcement officials, insurers, and other antifraud organizations.

Audit Trail: Regulators may ask insurers to demonstrate the traceability of data to ensure accuracy across all systems and processes, thereby ensuring the validity and consistency of data.

Auto Insurance Working Group: A working group within the Auto Insurance (C/D) Working Group of the Property and Casualty Insurance Committee and the Market Regulation and Consumer Affairs Committee to:

- Review issues and make recommendations relating to low-income households and the auto insurance marketplace.
- Consider the collection of data to evaluate the availability and affordability of auto insurance.

Big Data Working Group: A committee within the Innovation and Technology Task Force at NAIC Big Data Working Group whose function is to:

- Review the regulatory frameworks used to oversee insurers' use of consumer and non-insurance data, and recommends possible improvements.
- Propose a mechanism to facilitate states' ability to conduct technical analysis of, and to collect data, related to states' review of complex models used by insurers for underwriting, rating, and claims.
- Assess the data needs and the tools required for state insurance regulators to monitor the marketplace and evaluate underwriting, rating, claims, and marketing practices.

Data Dictionary: Describes all data elements and metadata used to meet reporting requirements, including establishing data standards for dates, allowed values, and codes.

File and Use Laws: A regulatory policy where an insurer must submit a filing (according to guidelines provided by the jurisdiction) before implementation.

Financial data: Insurers must report financial data to regulators about periodical and current financial status. Regulators use financial data to evaluate financial solvency and decide whether to take regulatory action to conserve an insurer's assets and protect the interests of policyholders.

Market Conduct Examination: Regulators use market conduct examinations to review a company's practices in relation to a state's unfair and deceptive trade practices laws and regulations.

No File: A regulatory policy where a filing of forms and endorsements is not required, but the insurer must maintain documentation, in case the regulator requests it.

Prior Approval Law: A regulatory policy where the regulator must approve the policy form and endorsement language before insurers can use them in the state.

Rating Bureau: Rating bureaus also act as statistical agents and file rates or loss costs, rules and forms with insurance regulators.

Risk-Based Capital: Insurance regulators use Risk-Based Capital (RBC) standards to assess an insurer's financial strength and determine whether it has sufficient capital to meet its obligations.

Special calls: Need for additional statistical data over established reporting requirements, sometimes for a relatively short period of time or due to unforeseeable data needs, possibly due to legislative, political, or consumer pressures.

Statistical Agents: Some advisory organizations are statistical agents that collect statistical data from insurers, allowing them to meet the requirement to report statistics to insurance regulators.

Statistical Data: Regulators use statistical data to evaluate the rates and rating structures used by insurers in a state.

Statistical Data Monitoring System: A set of procedures to control the quality of data for certain lines of insurance.

Statistical Data Working Group: A working group within the Casualty Actuarial and Statistical Task Force at NAIC to provide updates to the *Statistical Handbook of Data available to Insurance Regulators.* It also updates, provides technical assistance, and oversees the production of several annual reports that assist regulators in monitoring markets.

Trade associations: Associations formed to advocate for their members with insurance regulators and legislators.

Use and File: A regulatory policy where jurisdictions allow insurers to implement forms and endorsements before filing with the jurisdiction.

Review Questions

1. **Describe the role of licensing in state insurance regulation.**

All jurisdictions have licensing guidelines that require insurers, agents, and brokers, and some also license staff, independent, and public adjusters to do business within the state. Licensing guidelines are designed to meet and maintain the state's regulatory requirements that protect consumers. Each state maintains a database of licensees, tracking violations and other activities. Additionally, NAIC maintains databases for producer licensing information. Regulators use these databases primarily to track compliance with the state's laws and regulations, and the public uses them to verify and research licensed professionals.

2. **How do regulators ensure clarity and consistency among insurers?**

State insurance regulators have the authority to approve policy language in forms, endorsements, and rates, which are enforced through various filing regulations. Some regulators require insurers to defer to the forms/endorsements/rates developed by an advisory organization.

3. **What are some ways that regulators protect insurance consumers?**

Regulators control the licensing and approval of the rates, forms and endorsements. They conduct market conduct examinations to regulate the activities of organizations in the interests of fairness and consumer protection.

4. **How do regulators facilitate affordable and available coverage?**

State laws require three standards for rates: they may not be inadequate, excessive or unfairly discriminatory. Fair discrimination, which results in rates that differ based on each insured's level of risk, increases insurers' willingness to write business, and is allowed.

5. **What are some methods available to regulators to maintain the financial solvency of insurance companies?**

Using both statistical and financial data, regulators receive several reports from the NAIC that help them understand market trends, cost trends, and potential difficulties insurers or consumers may face. They monitor the financial strength, stability, and liquidity of insurers and the early warning signs of insurers' inability to meet financial responsibilities, including ethical conduct arising from such a condition.

6. Explain the difference between financial data and statistical data.

The financial data that insurers must report focuses on quarterly or annual performance as well as current financial status. Regulators use this financial data as a snapshot view of a financial picture. With this kind of information, regulators evaluate an insurer's financial solvency and decide whether to take regulatory action to conserve the insurer's assets and protect policyholders' interests. Regulators use statistical data to evaluate the rates and rating structures used by insurers in a state. Statistical data facilitates regulators with the necessary analysis of premiums and losses on a comparative basis amongst insurers.

7. Outline the objective, features and benefits of the Statistical Data Monitoring System (SDMS).

The objective of the SDMS is to ensure the reliability of the Private Passenger Automobile data collection process that provides raw statistical data for statistical filings and ratemaking purposes. SDMS:

- Provides regulators with a measure of data accuracy.
- Provides statistical agents with the tools needed to monitor the quality of data received from each individual company and to develop a means to control the accuracy of their own operations.
- Provides the regulator with the tools to verify adherence by each company and statistical agent.
- Provides each company with the tools needed to control the accuracy of its own statistical data and to control errors compared with other companies.

8. Explain the reasons for a special call.

When the data collected is insufficient to answer key questions, or when legislative, political, or consumer pressures require additional statistical data, regulators issue a special call for data reporting.

9. Explain insurance regulators' concerns about data quality and possible solutions to those concerns.

The data received by the regulatory agency from the various insurers and statistical agents is similar but may not be the same with regard to quality, consistency, and reliability. This raises concerns among regulators about the data received, which in turn influences the confidence they place in it. Regulators address these concerns by standardizing the data and defining its completeness. Regulators may also ask insurers to demonstrate a full audit trail and to see the data dictionary.

10. Distinguish the regulation of workers compensation insurance from other lines of insurance.

For workers compensation insurance, the IAIABC and NCCI provide a framework of rates, policy forms, and reporting requirements that aid the regulators in regulating this line of insurance in their jurisdiction.

11. **What is the role of the International Association of Industrial Accident Boards and Commissions (IAIABC)?**

IAIABC is an association of workers' compensation regulators and industry professionals. The IAIABC enables regulators to share information to find solutions to reduce harm and aid recovery from injuries resulting from occupational accidents and illnesses on an international scale.

12. **How does the National Council on Compensation Insurance (NCCI) influence the workers compensation market?**

NCCI gathers data, analyzes industry trends, and provides objective insurance rate and loss cost recommendations for most jurisdictions. Thirty-two states have designated NCCI as their licensed rating and statistical organization.

Data Management at a
Life & Health Insurance Company

Educational Objectives

Upon completion of this assignment, you should be able to:

1.   Identify the unique characteristics of and terms used in life and health insurance.
2.   Identify the basic forms of life and health insurance and related products.
3.   Identify rating and underwriting variables considered in life and health insurance.
4.   Describe recent issues for life and health insurance related to data quality and data management.
5.   Explain the issues related to principles-based reserving in life insurance.
6.   Identify the major life and health insurance organizations.

For each assignment, define or describe each of the Key Terms and Concepts and answer each of the Review and Discussion Questions.

Key Terms and Concepts

American Council of Life Insurers (ACLI):

America's Health Insurance Plans (AHIP):

Annuities:

Beneficiary:

Electronic health record (EHR) or Electronic medical record (EMR):

Fee-for-service:

Health Information Technology for Economic and Clinical Health Act (HITECH Act):

Health Insurance Portability and Accountability Act (HIPAA):

Health Maintenance Organization (HMO):

High-Deductible Health plans (HDHP):

Insurable interest:

Insured:

LIMRA (Life Insurance and Market Research Association):

Life Statistical Services (LSS):

LOMA:

Long-term care insurance:

Medical Information Bureau (MIB):

Medical underwriting:

Mortality table:

National Association of Health Underwriters (NAHU):

National Alliance of Life Companies (NALC):

Point of Service (POS):

Policy Anniversary:

Policy owner or Policyholder:

Preferred Provider Organization (PPO):

Qualified health insurance plan:

Rider:

Term life insurance policy:

Whole life insurance policy:

Universal life insurance:

Variable life insurance:

Review Questions

1. Identify the unique characteristics of and terms used in life and health insurance.

2. How are property/casualty and life/health insurance data collection efforts similar?

3. How are property/casualty and life/health insurance data collection not similar?

4. Given the differences between property/casualty and life/health data, what is a main concern for life/health data managers?

5. For group health insurance, why is it more important to collect the state where the insurer lives rather than the state where the insurance is purchased?

6. How can dates be important for certain health care policies?

7. How might when and where an incident occurred affect which insurance policy provides coverage?

8. What are the terms used in life/health and property/casualty to describe contract amendments?

9. How can some life/health insurance policies be similar to property/casualty policies with respect to terms of coverage?

10. How can some life/health insurance policies be dissimilar to property/casualty policies with respect to terms of coverage?

11. How are the terms policyholder/policy owner, insured and beneficiary used differently for life/health than for property/casualty insurance?

12. Provide some examples of why defining policy owner, insured, and beneficiary can be complicated.

13. How do policy owner, insured and beneficiary differ between individual and group health policies?

14. What is a sometime exception to this rule related to accidental death and dismemberment insurance?

15. How does life insurance determine insurable interest?

16. List the most common forms of life insurance.

17. What is the most common and basic form of life insurance sold?

18. Describe the characteristics of term life insurance.

19. For whom is term life insurance most advantageous?

20. What type of protection does whole life insurance provide?

21. How does whole life insurance differ from term life?

22. List the two basic types of whole life insurance.

23. Identify some characteristics of ordinary whole life insurance.

24. How is the premium for ordinary whole life insurance calculated?

25. How does the premium of ordinary whole life insurance compare to term life?

26. Why will the total of all premiums paid under whole and term policies will be roughly equal if the policies remain in force for the insured's average life expectancy, at least theoretically?

27. What are some of the benefits of the cash value component of whole life policies?

28. How does limited-payment whole life insurance differ from ordinary whole life insurance?

29. How does universal life insurance differ from whole life?

30. How does universal life insurance offer flexibility to the policyholder?

31. How does universal life work as both an investment and insurance instrument?

32. What is the benefit to policyholders of universal life insurance with respect to premium payments?

33. What option does universal life offer regarding policy limits?

34. What does universal life with secondary guarantees offer to policyholders?

35. What concern lead to the development of ULSG policies?

36. What does the secondary guarantee ensure?

37. How does variable life insurance differ from other life insurance policies?

38. How does variable life insurance work?

39. What is the concern for policyholders with variable life insurance?

40. As a result of the investment component of variable life insurance, who regulates these products?

41. Are annuities a form of life insurance, and what is their purpose?

42. How does an annuity work?

43. How are annuities used to provide financial security?

44. How do fixed annuities and variable annuities differ?

45. How does regulation of health insurance differ from other insurance?

46. What law mandates minimum standard benefits for health insurance?

47. What is a qualified health insurance plan?

48. How has the term qualified health insurance plan evolved over time?

49. Identify examples of types of insurance which may be considered health insurance but are not qualified plans.

50. Identify the types of health insurance plans.

51. Describe how a fee-for-service plan works.

52. Which two health insurance plans are managed care plans?

53. Identify the characteristics of a preferred provider organization.

54. Identify the characteristics of a health maintenance organization.

55. Which type of health insurance plan combines features from both PPOs and HMOs?

56. How does a point of service plan work?

57. How does a high-deductible health plan benefit consumers?

58. What is the benefit of pairing a HDHP with a Health Savings Accounts?

59. Is long-term care insurance a type of life or health insurance?

60. What is long-term care insurance?

61. Why is health insurance not intended to provide long-term care coverage?

62. Does Medicare cover long-term care expenses?

63. What is covered under long-term care insurance?

64. Identify the two forms of long-term care insurance?

65. How do reimbursement and indemnity long-term care policies differ?

66. How does the information collected to life/health insurers differ from that collected by property/casualty insurers?

67. Provide examples of how the amount and type of information collected about insured differs by coverage.

68. When is dependency status a key element for some health insurance?

69. What factors help determine dependency status and thus are tracked by insurers?

70. How do life insurers classify applicants?

71. What are mortality tables?

72. What is the basis of mortality tables?

73. How do insurers use mortality tables?

74. What is the difference between public and private mortality tables?

75. In addition to age, what other types of information do life insurers collect and evaluate to determine whether or not they want to insure the individual, and, if so, how to classify and rate the applicant compared to others in the same age group?

76. What is medical underwriting?

77. How does the Affordable Care Act impact medical underwriting?

78. What factors may health insurers consider in rating a policy?

79. Why is where the insured lives a concern for pricing coverage?

80. How does consideration of loss experience for an entire group affect individual insureds?

81. Although the ACA prohibits health insurers from considering the applicant's build (e.g., weight) as an underwriting and rating factor, under what conditions can employees be required to pay higher premiums?

82. What is the purpose of the Health Insurance Portability and Accountability Act (HIPAA)?

83. What Insurers must comply with the provisions of HIPAA?

84. What covered entities (CE) must follow standards and operational rules per the Administrative Simplification provisions of HIPAA?

85. Per HIPAA's Privacy Rule and the Security Rule what is protected?

86. What is the term used by The Privacy Rule to describe this information?

87. What are two issues addressed by The Privacy Rule?

88. List some of the areas covered in The Privacy Rule's administrative requirements for covered entities.

89. What is the purpose of the HIPAA Security Rule?

90. How are these safeguards categorized?

91. What is included in administrative safeguards?

92. What do physical safeguards control?

93. What is included in technical safeguards?

94. How have states responded to the issues of privacy and security?

95. What does California's Insurance Information and Privacy Protection Act (IIPPA) require of agents, brokers, or insurance companies?

96. What is the Health Information Technology for Economic and Clinical Health Act?

97. Why are electronic health records (EHR) preferred to paper records?

98. Describe how an EHR improves care for a patient.

99. What is intended benefits of the HITECH Act?

100. With respect to EHRs, what is the focus of meaningful use?

101. What does the HITECH Act include to support the five health care priorities?

102. How does the HITECT Act expand HIPPAA privacy provisions?

103. What is medical theft?

104. How does medical theft affect the insured?

105. How does medical theft affect the health insurance company?

106. List the ways companies depend on accurate data for day-to-day and strategic operations.

107.   How do life and health companies use data for marketing and advertising purposes?

108.   What is the effect of incorrect information for marketing and advertising purposes?

109.   Why is accurate data crucial for rating?

110.   What is the concern of using incorrect information for rating?

111.   How does accurate data help claims processing?

112.   Why does an insurer need accurate data to evaluate product offerings?

113.   What is the most prevalent form of insurance fraud today?

114.   How does accurate data help insurers fight fraud?

115.   How does medical fraud affect the cost of insurance?

116.   How do life insurers plan to use big data and predictive analytics?

117.   What are the top barriers to using big data and predictive analytics?

118.   What are the top challenges to using big data and predictive analytics?

119.   What types of data were collected by the majority of life companies?

120.   What types of data are collected and used by fewer companies?

121.   How might analytics be used by health insurers?

122.   How might the popularity of personal fitness and smart watches be used by health insurers?

123.   What other types of data can be analyzed to predict health care costs?

124.   How does the ACA affect insurers ability to use big data and predictive analytics?

125.   How are health care insurers using data analytics to reduce or prevent claim costs?

126.   Beginning in 2020, what method will life insurers be required to use to estimate financial statement reserves for l term and universal life with secondary guarantees?

127.   What is the difference in reserving between property/casualty and life insurance?

128.   How did insurers set reserves prior to principle-based reserving?

129.   What is the assumption underlying these historical rules?

130.   What does principle-based reserving consider to support more accurate reserving?

131.   What technique is used to estimate reserves under principle-based reserving?

132.   What factors will companies consider in determining reserves?

133.   What precipitated the move from standard valuation methods to principle-based valuation?

134.   What is the purpose of the NAIC's model Standard Valuation Law (SVL)?

135.   List the stated goals of the Valuation Manual.

136.   Which sections of the Valuation Manual focus on Experience Reporting Requirements?

137.   How does the Experience Reporting Requirements' uniform reporting structure assist with the move to principle-based reserving?

138.   What is the purpose of Section VM-50?

139.   What additional changes does the Experience Reporting Requirements call for?

140.   What is the purpose of Section VM-51?

141.   What changes will principle-based reserving require of life insurance data managers?

142.   If life insurers offer products to which principle-based rules do not apply, what may they need to do?

143.   What are the challenges to data managers in a life company as principal-based reserving is implemented?

144.   Identify some of the conditions that result in unclaimed benefits from life insurance policies.

145.   How have states addressed the issue of unclaimed benefits?

146.   What does NCOIL's model Unclaimed Life Insurance Act require?

147.   What information does the Social Security Administration's Death Master File (DMF) include?

148.   The NCOIL Model Act requires insurers to implement "fuzzy match" criteria, which may be challenging for some companies. List the conditions that insurers' search procedures must consider.

149.   Identify organizations that support the business of life and health insurers.

150.   Which of these organizations are trade organizations?

151.   How does LOMA support the life insurance industry?

152. What is the Fellow Life Management Institute (FMLI) designation?

153. How does LIMRA support the life insurance industry?

154. What is LL Global, Inc.?

155. Identify the types of coverage provided by member companies of the American Council of Life Insurers (ACLI).

156. How does ACLI support the life insurance industry?

157. What types of companies are served by the National Alliance of Life Companies (NALC)?

158. How does the NALC support its member companies?

159. Why was the NALC created?

160. Who is represented by the National Association of Health Underwriters (NAHU)?

161.   How does the National Association of Health Underwriters (NAHU) support its members?

162.   Identify the organizations that rely on voluntarily reported data from life and health insurance companies.

163.   How is data from these organizations used?

164.   Identify America's Health Insurance Plans (AHIP).

165.   Identify the entities that can join America's Health Insurance Plans (AHIP).

166.   What types of data are collected by AHIP from its members?

167.   What is the focus of the Medical Information Bureau (MIB)?

168.   How does the Medical Information Bureau (MIB) differ from other major life and health insurance organizations?

169.   Who are MIB's members?

170.   What information services does MIB offer its members?

171.   What function does the Life Statistical Services (LSS) serve to members?

Answers to Assignment 12 Questions

NOTE: These answers are provided to give students a basic understanding of acceptable types of responses. They are often not the only valid answers and are not intended to provide an exhaustive response to the questions.

Key Terms and Concepts

American Council of Life Insurers (ACLI): The ACLI is an advocacy organization representing the interests of its member companies in state, federal, and international public policy issues and provides members with life insurance, annuities, retirement plans, long-term care, disability income insurance, and reinsurance.

America's Health Insurance Plans (AHIP): AHIP is a national trade association established to represent the interests of health insurers writing group benefits. AHIP members include health care consultants, attorneys, insurance agents and brokers, practitioners, and educators.

Annuities: Financial vehicles used for financial planning or retirement purposes.

Beneficiary: The recipient of policy proceeds.

Electronic health record (EHR) or Electronic medical record (EMR): Patient medical data that is stored electronically is known as an electronic health record (EHR), also referred to as an electronic medical record (EMR).

Fee-for-service: A term in healthcare insurance plan in which the insured is free to choose where to obtain care.

Health Information Technology for Economic and Clinical Health Act (HITECH Act): The HITECH Act provides direction in the use and protection of electronic protected health information (ePHI).

Health Insurance Portability and Accountability Act (HIPAA): HIPAA includes the Privacy Rule and the Security Rule, which provide definitions and guidance on the transmission of personally identifiable information.

Health Maintenance Organization (HMO): An HMO is a type of managed care plan in which an insurance company has contracted with "in-network" providers, and the insured must select from an in-network list of doctors.

High-Deductible Health plans (HDHP): HDHP is a type of health insurance plan where the insured has a much higher deductible than under other types of health insurance plans in exchange for comparatively lower premiums.

Insurable interest: A legal term in an insurance policy, meaning a person or entity should stand to suffer a financial loss if and when an event against the insured occurs.

Insured: The person whose death or disability will trigger coverage.

LOMA (Life Office Management Association): LOMA is an international trade association for the life insurance industry that administers training and education programs for insurers related to the business and operation of life insurance.

LIMRA (Life Insurance and Market Research Association): LIMRA is an international trade organization that provides members (life insurance companies) with research and market insight to assist members with business strategies.

Life Statistical Services (LSS): A division under the MIB that functions as a statistical reporting agency.

Long-term care insurance: Provides financial support in the event that the insured requires on-going care for such things as temporary part-time assistance with daily activities to full time nursing home care.

Medical Information Bureau (MIB): The MIB is considered a consumer reporting agency for healthcare data with main focus on fraud prevention.

Medical underwriting: Medical underwriting the process of evaluating information related to an applicant for health insurance to determine insurability and rates.

Mortality table: This is a table showing mortality rates for each age. Mortality rate tables depict the probability that a person will die during the following year. Insurers use mortality tables to determine premium rates and establish loss reserves.

National Association of Health Underwriters (NAHU): The NAHU is a advocacy organization for health insurance agents, brokers, and employee benefit professionals in state and federal public policy issues, and provides extensive educational and networking opportunities.

National Alliance of Life Companies (NALC): NALC is a trade association formed to serve the interests of small- to mid-sized companies in public policy matters. The NALC also includes health writers among its members.

Point of Service (POS): A POS is a type of healthcare plan that combines features of both PPOs and HMOs, wherein the insurer establishes a network of preferred providers, but the insured also has the option to seek care outside of the network.

Policy Anniversary: The date on which the life insurance policy's annual review will take place and from which the premiums are calculated.

Policy owner or Policyholder: The person (or business) who purchased the policy.

Preferred Provider Organization (PPO): A PPO is a type of managed healthcare plan in which the plan establishes contracts with medical providers and encourages insureds to use in-network service providers.

Qualified health insurance plan: A comprehensive health insurance plan that provides the mandated essential benefits, follows the set limits on insured cost-sharing (such as deductibles, copayments, and maximum out-of-pocket payments), and meets other requirements of the Affordable Care Act, is considered a qualified health insurance plan.

Rider: The contract amendment that may add or exclude coverage, or amend terms and conditions of the underlying contract.

Term life insurance policy: Term policies provide coverage only while they are in force and for the term of the policy.

Whole life insurance policy: Provides permanent, lifetime protection.

Universal life insurance: Universal life insurance is a variation of whole life insurance that combines life insurance and savings under a single flexible plan.

Variable life insurance: Variable life insurance is a type of permanent life insurance that includes an investment component.

Review Questions

1. Identify the unique characteristics of and terms used in life and health insurance.

While there are major differences in the business and regulation of life and health insurance compared to property and casualty insurance, the main differences for a data manager are the major organizations important to the life and health insurance lines. A data manager must be particularly alert about sharing personally identifiable information only with authorized sources.

2. How are property/casualty and life/health insurance data collection efforts similar?

As with property and casualty data, life and health data is collected and tracked on the owner of the policy, the policy coverage, coverage exclusions and optional coverages, and — with respect to health insurance —deductibles.

3. How are property/casualty and life/health insurance data collection not similar?

There may be significant differences with respect to the age of the data, and the ability to obtain additional data after policy issuance. Typically, property and casualty policies are renewed and paid for annually, which enables the company to obtain updated information from the insured — helping ensure that data and information are current. However, some life insurance policies, annuities, and some specialized health insurance policies can continue to renew or remain in force for years, without coverage changes or even contact (other than receipt of premiums) with the customer, until a claim for benefits is made.

4. **Given the differences between property/casualty and life/health data, what is a main concern for life/health data managers? [EO 1]**

For life/health policies, data managers need to be aware of the potential limitations of existing data and need to work with other company divisions to help ensure that data are as current and accurate as possible.

5. **For group health insurance, why is it more important to collect the state where the insurer lives rather than the state where the insurance is purchased? [EO 1]**

In group health insurance, especially group medical insurance, it is important to consider where the insured individual lives. This is because some states have laws regarding the coverage provided individuals living in their state, regardless of the state in which the insurance policy was issued. These are known as extraterritorial states.

6. **How can dates be important for certain health care policies? [EO 1]**

Dates are important for administering time-based limits on certain health care services. For example, dental insurance often limits dental cleanings to twice each year.

7. **How might when and where an incident occurred affect which insurance policy provides coverage? [EO 1]**

In the case of health insurance, it is important to know whether the disability was work-related, as if it were, the claim may be more appropriately covered under workers' compensation insurance rather than health insurance.

8. **What are the terms used in life/health and property/casualty to describe contract amendments? [EO 1]**

The term "rider" is commonly used in life and health contracts instead of the property and casualty term "endorsement" to describe contract amendments that may add or exclude coverage or amend terms and conditions of the underlying contract.

9. **How can some life/health insurance policies be similar to property/casualty policies with respect to terms of coverage? [EO 1]**

Health insurance policies and many life insurance policies are written for a specific term of coverage — generally one year. Like property and casualty policies, these life and health policies may be renewed with different terms, conditions, or premiums — and will lapse if the renewal premium is not paid.

10. How can some life/health insurance policies be dissimilar to property/casualty policies with respect to terms of coverage? [EO 1]

Some life insurance policies are intended to remain active unless all policy benefits are paid or the policy is cancelled by the policy owner. Anniversary dates mark these policies.

11. How are the terms policyholder/policy owner, insured and beneficiary used differently for life/health than for property/casualty insurance? [EO 1]

The life insurance policy owner or policyholder is the person (or business) who purchased the policy; the "insured" is the person whose death or disability will trigger coverage; and the beneficiary is the recipient of policy proceeds. Commonly, the policy owner and insured will be the same person and the beneficiary another person; or the owner and beneficiary will be the same person and the person insured will be another person.

12. Provide some example of why defining policy owner, insured and beneficiary can be complicated. [EO 1]

- A mother who purchases life insurance on herself to protect her children will be both the policy owner and the insured, and her children are the beneficiaries.
- If the same woman purchases a policy to insure the life of her husband to protect herself, she will be both the policy owner and the beneficiary.
- Suppose several years after the policy is issued, the wife changes the beneficiary to be her child. In this case, the policy owner, insured, and beneficiary are three different individuals.

13. How do policy owner, insured and beneficiary differ between individual and group health policies? [EO 1]

In individual health insurance policies, the policyholder, insured, and beneficiary are typically the same—an individual who purchases a health insurance policy on himself is the policyholder, the subject of the insurance, and the beneficiary of benefits. However, in group health insurance, the employer or association that purchases the coverage is the policy owner. Still, the employees or association members, and perhaps their families, are the insureds and beneficiaries.

14. What is sometime exception to this rule related to accidental death and dismemberment insurance? [EO 1]

The accidental dismemberment portion of this insurance coverage classifies it as health insurance rather than life insurance. Upon accidental loss of a limb or an eye, the insured would receive an insurance payment. Of course, upon the accidental death of the insured, it would be impossible for the insured to collect the policy proceeds; therefore, as in life insurance, a beneficiary is named.

15. How does life insurance determine insurable interest? [EO 1]

First, it extends insurable interest to include close family relationships. A non-working spouse has a strong insurable interest in a working spouse; however, this relationship is not as strong between a parent who insures the life of a child. Second, due to the long-term nature of life insurance, the insurable interest only has to exist at the inception of the policy. This allows for ownership of a policy to be "assigned" or transferred to another individual or entity. This transfer of ownership must follow insurance company guidelines and be duly recorded by the insurer.

16. List the most common forms of life insurance. [EO 2]

- Term life insurance.
- Ordinary whole life insurance.
- Limited whole life insurance.
- Universal life insurance.
- Universal life policies with secondary guarantees (ULSG).
- Variable life insurance.

17. What is the most common and basic form of life insurance sold? [EO 2]

Term life insurance is the most common and basic form of life insurance sold.

18. Describe the characteristics of term life insurance. [EO 2]

Term policies provide coverage only while the policy is in force. If the policy owner fails to pay the premium, coverage ends. Term policies do not have a savings component and do not build cash value. Additionally, premiums may change at each renewal and increase as the insured ages.

19. For whom is term life insurance most advantageous? [EO 2]

Term life insurance is particularly advantageous for younger individuals as it provides a relatively inexpensive way to purchase immediate protection for dependents.

20. What type of protection does whole life insurance provide? [EO 2]

Whole life insurance is intended to provide permanent, lifetime protection.

21. How does whole life insurance differ from term life? [EO 12]

Whole life insurance also includes an investment component and will accrue cash values.

22. List the two basic types of whole life insurance. [EO 2]

The two basic types of whole life insurance are ordinary whole life and limited payment whole life.

23. Identify some characteristics of ordinary whole life insurance. [EO 2]

Ordinary whole life insurance policy benefits are payable immediately; the premiums do not increase with age; and the policy will be considered paid in full if or when the insured reaches a stated age – usually 95 or 100.

24. How is the premium for ordinary whole life insurance calculated? [EO 2]

The premium is calculated based on the insured's age at the time of purchase and is calculated based on mortality tables.

25. How does the premium of ordinary whole life insurance compare to term life? [EO 2]

Because the premium doesn't increase, the policy owner will generally pay more for the coverage at the time of purchase then he or she would for the same limit of term coverage — at least initially.

26. Why will the total of all premiums paid under whole and term policies be roughly equal if the policies remain in force for the insured's average life expectancy, at least theoretically? [EO 2]

Because mortality costs increase as the insured ages, the level premium includes both a mortality charge and an additional loading, which funds the policy's cash value. As the insured ages, the amount of the total premium going toward the cost of the insurance increases, and the amount going into the cash side decreases.

27. What are some of the benefits of the cash value component of whole life policies? [EO 2]

If the policy owner elects to give up the policy, he or she is entitled to the policy's cash value. Money accrued in the cash value portion of the policy can also be used as a loan by the insured or to pay insurance costs if premium payments aren't made. If the insured dies, however, the cash value is not payable to beneficiaries, but is retained by the company.

28. How does limited payment whole life insurance differ from ordinary whole life? [EO 2]

Limited payment whole life insurance differs in that the policies can be issued with stated premium periods or with the intent that coverage will be paid for ("paid up") when the insured reaches a certain age.

29. How does universal life insurance differ from whole life? [EO 2]

Universal life insurance is a variation of whole life insurance that combines life insurance and savings under a single flexible plan.

30. How does universal life insurance offer flexibility to the policyholder? [EO 2]

After the policy is purchased, the policy owner may increase or decrease the death benefit amount and may vary the premium payments, provided the minimum premium requirements are paid.

31. How does universal life work as both an investment and insurance instrument? [EO 2]

The policy owner pays premiums into a cash value account. The policy owner has no say in how the cash value is invested, but does earn interest at a guaranteed minimum rate. The insurance coverage costs and company expenses are then deducted from the cash account.

32. What is the benefit to policyholders of universal life insurance with respect to premium payments? [EO 2]

The policy owner has the option to increase, decrease, or even skip premium payments. If premiums are skipped, the cost of the insurance is paid from the cash value account.

33. What option does universal life offer regarding policy limit? [EO 2]

Universal life insurance policies may be written with an increasing death benefit policy or as a level benefit policy. With an increasing death benefit option, the accrued cash value is added to the death benefit. With a level benefit policy, as the cash value account increases, the amount of pure insurance protection decreases.

34. What does universal life with secondary guarantees offer to policyholders? [EO 2]

Universal life policies with secondary guarantees (ULSG) offer a secondary guarantee: a death benefit for a stated period of time.

35. What concern lead to the development of ULSG policies? [EO 2]

Secondary guarantees arose to ensure that the life insurance would remain in force even if the cash value is zero – a possibility if insurance costs increase due to changes in mortality costs or decreases in insurer investment experience (i.e. decreasing interest rates).

36. What does the secondary guarantee ensure? [EO 2]

Without the secondary guarantee feature, if the full insurance premium was not paid, the policy would lapse.

37. How does variable life insurance differ from other life insurance policies? [EO 2]

Variable life insurance is a type of permanent life insurance that includes an investment component. Although considered life insurance, universal life products are also marketed and sold as investments.

38. How does variable life insurance work? [EO 2]

The cash value is placed into a separate account that is maintained by the insurance company but the policy owner can chose how the premiums will be invested. Cash value funds are invested in securities, and the insurer doesn't offer a minimum guaranteed return.

39. What is the concern for policyholders with variable life insurance? [EO 2]

The cash value may increase or decrease, and the policy owner, not the company, shoulders the risk.

40. As a result of the investment component of variable life insurance, who regulates these products? [EO 2]

State insurance departments regulate variable life insurance as an insurance product, and the Securities and Exchange Commission (SEC) treats it as a security.

41. Are annuities a form of life insurance, and what is their purpose? [EO 2]

Although many life insurance companies offer annuities, annuities are not life insurance – they are vehicles used for financial planning or retirement purposes.

42. How does an annuity work? {EO 2]

An annuity is a contract whereby the policy owner deposits a sum of money with the issuing company and the company, in turn, agrees to provide an income to the annuitant (the person who collects the benefits) beginning at a stated time, and for a stated duration.

43. How are annuities used to provide financial security? [EO 2]

Annuities are often used to protect the annuitant from outliving their savings.

44. How do fixed annuities and variable annuities differ? [EO 2]

A fixed annuity pays a fixed principle amount; while the principle payment under a variable annuity may vary depending on the investment performance of deposited funds.

45. How does regulation of health insurance differ from other insurance? [EO 2]

Like other forms of insurance, health insurance is regulated at the state level; however, states are required to adhere to the requirements of federal law.

46. What law mandates minimum standard benefits for health insurance? [EO 2]

The Patient Protection and Affordable Care Act (also referred to as the Affordable Care Act, ACA, or "Obamacare") mandates minimum essential health insurance benefits.

47. What is a qualified health insurance plan? [EO 2]

A health insurance plan that provides the mandated essential benefits, follows the set limits on insured cost-sharing (such as deductibles, copayments, and maximum out-of-pocket payments) and meets other requirements of the Affordable Care Act, is considered a qualified health insurance plan.

48. How has the term qualified health insurance plan evolved over time? [EO 2]

A qualified plan was originally intended to distinguish those plans that met the health insurance mandate under the Affordable Care Act. Today, the term is more commonly used to describe a comprehensive healthcare insurance plan.

49. Identify examples of types of insurance which may be considered health insurance but are not qualified plans. [EO 2]

Examples of non-qualified health insurance include dental insurance, vision insurance, short-term medical insurance, Medicare supplement insurance, and accident-only insurance.

50. Identify the types of health insurance plans. [EO 2]

- Fee-for-service.
- Preferred Provider Organization (PPO).
- Health Maintenance Organization (HMO).
- Point of Service (POS).
- High-Deductible Health Plans (HDHP).

51. Describe how a fee-for-service plan works. [EO 2]

In a fee-for-service plan, all medical services are considered separate expenses, and the medical provider or the insured is reimbursed by the company after a claim is filed.

52. Which two health insurance plans are managed care plans? [EO 2]

- Preferred Provider Organization (PPO).
- Health Maintenance Organization (HMO).

53. Identify the characteristics of a preferred provider organization. [EO 2]

PPOs are a type of managed care plan in which the plan establishes contracts with medical providers. Typically, in-network providers have agreed to reimbursement rates established by the insurer. The insured is free to visit the healthcare provider of his or her choice without referral from a primary care physician, but the insurance company encourages the use of "in network" providers by offering higher benefits or lower costs for "in network" providers.

54. Identify the characteristics of a health maintenance organization. [EO 2]

HMOs are also managed care plans with contracted "in network" providers. Insureds are required to select a primary care doctor from within the network, and that doctor acts as a gatekeeper —coordinating all of the insured's care and providing referrals to other care providers as needed. Insureds are encouraged to obtain care within the plan in exchange for low out-of-pocket costs and low (or no) deductibles. If care is obtained outside the network, the insurance company may not provide coverage, and if it does, the insured will have higher out-of-pocket costs.

55. Which type of health insurance plan combines features from both PPOs and HMOs? [EO 2]

A point of service plan combines features of both PPOs and HMOs.

56. How does a point of service plan work? [EO 2]

The insurer establishes a network of preferred providers, but the insured can also seek care outside the network. Care received out of network is subject to different coverage terms similar to traditional fee-for-service plans.

57. How does a high-deductible health plan benefit consumers? [EO 2]

Under high-deductible health plans, the insured has a much higher deductible than under other types of health insurance plans in exchange for comparatively lower premiums.

58. What is the benefit of pairing an HDHP with a Health Savings Account? [EO 2]

These plans are often combined with Health Savings Accounts – savings accounts in which pre-tax income may be set aside for medical expenses.

59. Is long-term care insurance a type of life or health insurance? [EO 2]

Long-term care insurance may also be offered by life or health insurance companies, but does not fall under the umbrella of either life or health insurance.

60. What is long-term care insurance? [EO 2]

Long-term care insurance is intended to provide funding if the insured requires ongoing care, ranging from temporary, part-time assistance with daily activities to full-time nursing home care.

61. Why is health insurance not intended to provide long-term care coverage? [EO 2]

Unless the insured is receiving actual medical care, health insurance is not intended to cover the expense of long-term care.

62. Does Medicare cover long-term care expenses? [EO 2]

Medicare also does not cover long-term care expenses.

63. What is covered under long-term care insurance? {EO 2]

Long-term care coverage is typically available for facility-based (e.g., nursing home) care only, home-based (and sometimes community-based) care only, or comprehensive coverage across any setting.

64. Identify the two forms of long-term care insurance. [EO 2]

These policies may be written on a reimbursement basis or an indemnity basis.

65. How do reimbursement and indemnity long-term care policies differ? [EO 2]

A reimbursement policy pays for the actual costs of care, up to specified limits in the policy. An indemnity policy pays a specific amount for services, regardless of the actual expense billed. For example, a long-term care indemnity policy that provides a daily limit for care would pay that amount per day even if the actual expense was higher or lower than the stated benefit amount.

66. How does the information collected to life/health insurers differ from that collected by property/casualty insurers? [EO3]

More so than property and casualty insurance, information collected by life and health insurers can be very personal to the insured. Information transmitted for the purpose of processing health claims may be particularly sensitive.

67. Provide examples of how the amount and type of information collected about insureds differ by coverage. [EO 3]

- Underwriters use some of this information to assess the risk involved in insuring the individual. For example, certain occupations are considered extremely high risk for life and health coverages.
- The claims area also uses other information to validate the claim and determine payment. When paying a long-term disability claim, for example, it is necessary to determine whether the definition of disability contained in the policy is met (i.e., can the individual perform the tasks necessary to their profession).
- In certain types of health insurance, such as major medical, dental, or vision, coverage is extended to close family members and dependents—generally the spouse and children.

68. When is dependency status a key element for some health insurance? [EO 3]

Dependency status is a key element, not only at the time the insurance is issued, but also at the time a claim is made.

69. What factors help determine dependency status and thus are tracked by insurers? [EO 3]

Factors such as marital status, age, student status, and physical and/or mental disabilities help determine dependency status and, therefore, must be noted and tracked by the insurer.

70. How do life insurers classify applicants? [EO 3]

Life insurers classify applicants primarily by the insured's age, using mortality tables.

71. What are mortality tables? [EO 3]

The International Risk Management Institute(IRMI) defines and describes a mortality table as "a table showing mortality rates for each age."

72. What is the basis of mortality tables? [EO 3]

Mortality rates shown in such a table are based on actuarial analysis and indicate the probability that a person of the age for which the rate applies will die in the following year.

73. How do insurers use mortality tables? [O 3]

Insurers use mortality tables to determine premium rates and establish loss reserves.

74. What is the difference between public and private mortality tables? [EO 3]

Public mortality tables include United States Life Tables, published using census data, or other tables prescribed for use by state law. Proprietary tables are those created by the insurer or a third party as a secondary rating tool.

75. In addition to age, what other types of information do life insurers collect and evaluate to determine whether or not they want to insure the individual, and, if so, how to classify and rate the applicant compared to others in the same age group. [EO 3]

- Sex.
- Overall health and physical condition.
- Build (i.e., height compared to weight).
- Health history.
- Family health history.
- Occupation.

- Area of residence (geographic location).
- Personal habits (e.g., smoking, drinking).
- Economic status.
- Hobbies (e.g., flying aircraft, participation in certain sports).
- Military service.

76. What is medical underwriting? [EO 3]

The term medical underwriting refers to the process of evaluating an applicant's health insurance information to determine insurability and rates.

77. How does the Affordable Care Act impact medical underwriting? [EO 3]

The Affordable Care Act enacted significant limitations on health insurers' use of medical underwriting to set rates and prohibits insurers from denying coverage for medical reasons. The Affordable Care Act also restricts health insurers' ability to apply gender-specific rating factors and limits rate differences between tiers.

78. What factors may health insurers consider in rating a policy? [EO 3]

- Insured's age.
- Whether or not the insured is a smoker.
- Whether the policy covers an individual or a family.
- The level of benefits offered.
- Where the insured lives.
- The loss experience of an entire group.

79. Why is where the insured lives a concern for pricing coverage? [EO 3]

Costs of health care services may vary considerably by location based on competition, cost of living, and state-specific laws or regulations.

80. How does consideration of loss experience for an entire group affect individual insureds? [EO 3]

Insurers may not adjust rates for specific insureds based on claim history; but may adjust rates when warranted for an entire class of risks.

81. **Although the ACA prohibits health insurers from considering the applicant's build (e.g., weight) as an underwriting and rating factor, under what conditions can employees be required to pay higher premiums? [EO 3]**

The Affordable Care Act does permit employers to require employees to pay a higher share of their group health premiums if certain wellness goals aren't met, including body mass index (BMI) goals.

82. **What is the purpose of the Health Insurance Portability and Accountability Act (HIPAA)? [EO 4]**

- Make it possible for individuals and families to transfer their health insurance coverage if they change employers.
- Prevent healthcare fraud.
- Protect the confidentiality of personal health information.

83. **What Insurers must comply with the provisions of HIPAA? [EO 4]**

Health insurers must continually monitor for compliance with HIPAA. Although life insurers may also collect and store health information about applicants and insureds, the HIPAA Act does not apply to them.

84. **What covered entities (CE) must follow standards and operational rules per the Administrative Simplification provisions of HIPAA? [EO 4]**

- Health plans (e.g., group health insurance, health maintenance organizations).
- Health care clearinghouses (e.g., billing services, re-pricing companies).
- Health care providers (e.g., physicians, surgeons, nurses, dentists).

85. **Per HIPAA's Privacy Rule and the Security Rule, what is protected? [EO 4]**

The Privacy Rule protects all individually identifiable health information held or transmitted by a covered entity or its business associate, in any form or media, whether electronic, paper, or oral.

86. **What is the term used by The Privacy Rule to describe this information? [EO 4]**

The Privacy Rule refers to this information as protected health information (PHI).

87. What are two issues addressed by The Privacy Rule? [EO 4]

The Privacy Rule outlines the circumstances in which a covered entity (CE) can disclose PHI and the permitted uses of PHI. In addition, the Privacy Rule outlines administrative requirements for covered entities in a number of areas.

88. List some of the areas covered in The Privacy Rule's administrative requirements for covered entities. [EO 4]

- Development and implementation of privacy policies.
- Appointment of a privacy officer.
- Training for employees in privacy policies and management to ensure compliance.
- Implementation of administrative, technical, and physical safeguards for PHI.
- A process whereby individuals can make a complaint about the CE's use of PHI.
- Documentation and retention of a CE's privacy policies.

89. What is the purpose of the HIPAA Security Rule? [EO 4]

The HIPAA Security Rule establishes standards for the safeguarding of protected health information that is created, stored, used, or transmitted in electronic form (e-PHI).

90. How are these safeguards categorized? [EO 4]

Safeguards are categorized as administrative, physical, and technical.

91. What is included in administrative safeguards? [EO 4]

Administrative safeguards include assigning responsibility for e-PHI security to an individual and providing employees with appropriate training.

92. What do physical safeguards control? [EO 4]

Physical safeguards control access to computers and other equipment and the data they contain.

93. What is included in technical safeguards? [EO 4]

Technical safeguards include, for example, passwords or other unique user identification, such as retina scans.

94. How have states responded to the issues of privacy and security? [EO 4]

A number of states have enacted legislation similar to HIPAA, and in some cases, the legislation is more stringent than HIPAA. In addition, some states have passed laws specifically addressing personally identifiable information (PII) in the insurance context.

95. What does California's Insurance Information and Privacy Protection Act (IIPPA) require of agents, brokers, or insurance companies? [EO 4]

Agents, brokers, and insurers are required to provide a Privacy Notice describing their policies and procedures to ensure the security and confidentiality of PII. The Privacy Notice must also describe the kinds of information that the agent, broker, or insurer will collect, with whom that information will be shared, and the individual's right to restrict the sharing of that information.

96. What is the Health Information Technology for Economic and Clinical Health Act? [EO 4]

The Health Information Technology for Economic and Clinical Health Act (known as the HITECH Act) was included in the federal American Recovery and Reinvestment Act of 2009. The HITECH Act is considered a significant step forward in the use and protection of electronic protected health information (ePHI).

97. Why are electronic health records (EHR) preferred to paper records? [EO 4]

EHRs represent the data collected from a patient (or patients) and are stored in digital format so they may be shared with other health care providers. The electronic format is more accurate than paper-based files and helps reduce overall healthcare costs.

98. Describe how an EHR improves care for a patient. [EO 4]

If a patient is referred to a specialist within a health care setting, the specialist can determine from the EHR which medical tests have already been completed and do not need to be repeated.

99. What is intended benefits of the HITECH Act? [EO 4]

- The HITECH Act creates incentives for the adoption of "meaningful use" of EHRs as records. Engage patients and families in their health.
- Improve care coordination.
- Improve population and public health.
- Ensure adequate privacy and security protection for personal health information.

100.   With respect to EHRs, what is the focus of meaningful use? [EO 4]

"Meaningful use" focuses on five stated healthcare public policy priorities: improving quality and safety, increasing efficiency, and reducing health disparities.

101.   What does the HITECH Act include to support the five health care priorities? [EO 4]

To support the five healthcare priorities, the law includes a comprehensive list of specific data that must be captured, procedures for sharing data with patients, and required capabilities for the transmission of data to public agencies (e.g., immunization registries).

102.   How does the HITECT Act expand HIPPAA privacy provisions? [EO 4]

The HITECH Act expands HIPAA privacy provisions by extending the privacy and security requirements of HIPAA to business associates of covered entities. The HITECH Act also requires entities covered by HIPAA to report data breaches affecting 500 or more individuals. Data breaches must be reported to the U.S. Department of Health and Human Services, to media outlets, and to individuals suspected of being affected by the breach.

103.   What is medical theft? [EO 4]

Medical theft (sometimes called medical identity theft) occurs when a person steals another's name and/or insurance information to receive care or obtain prescription medications.

104.   How does medical theft affect the insured? [EO 4]

Medical theft can result in unpaid medical bills for the victim; policy benefits or limits may be used up and coverage no longer available to the victim/insured; and the thief's medical history may be added to the victim's records.

105.   How does medical theft affect the health insurance company? [EO 4]

If the initial breach resulted from the insurer's handling of data, the company may be liable for resulting damages. Regardless of where the initial breach or theft occurs, medical identity theft results in the insurance company collecting inaccurate claims data.

106. **List the ways companies depend on accurate data for day-to-day and strategic operations. [EO 4]**

- Marketing and advertising.
- Rating.
- Claims.
- Product offerings.
- Fraud Identification.

107. **How do life and health companies use data for marketing and advertising purposes? [EO 4]**

Insurers use existing policy data to identify customers who might benefit from new or updated products, optional riders, or other changes. Companies will also examine demographic information to identify growth opportunities and direct advertising dollars to those locations, individuals, or geographic areas where they believe they can successfully compete.

108. **What is the effect of incorrect information for marketing and advertising purposes? [EO 4]**

If insurers rely on incorrect information, marketing budgets may not be used efficiently, and companies may not achieve profitable growth goals.

109. **Why is accurate data crucial for rating? [EO 4]**

Accurate data from both the insurer's internal files and external sources is critical to calculating rates that adequately cover losses and expenses, and are neither excessive nor unfairly discriminatory.

110. **What is the concern of using incorrect information for rating? [EO 4]**

Inaccurate information can lead to solvency concerns, inadequate reserving, and customer dissatisfaction.

111. **How does accurate data help claims processing? [EO 4]**

Accurate data helps expedite claim processing, leading to improved customer satisfaction, better compliance with regulatory claim payment timeframe requirements, and reduced company expenses.

112. **Why do insurers need accurate data to evaluate product offerings? [EO 4]**

Insurers need accurate data to evaluate their current product offerings and to determine when to expand, revise, or discontinue certain products. Data related to loss experience, take-up rates (the percentage of eligible policyholders who purchase the rider), economic trends, and disability rates could all be considered.

113.   What is the most prevalent form of insurance fraud today? [EO 4]

Health insurance fraud is the most prevalent form of insurance fraud.

114.   How does accurate data help insurers fight fraud? [EO 4]

Accurate data can help insurers to identify trends that may indicate suspected fraud, or data collection or processing issues that may be vulnerable to fraud.

115.   How does medical fraud affect the cost of insurance? [EO 4]

Medical fraud drives up the costs of health insurance with false and inflated claims and the added costs of fraud investigation.

116.   How do life insurers plan to use big data and predictive analytics? [EO 4]

Life insurance companies plan to increase their use of big data and predictive analytics to increase market share. Companies also plan to use big data and predictive analytics to improve their business model, expand customer relationships, improve targeted marketing to new customers, and improve internal performance management.

117.   What are the top barriers to using big data and predictive analytics? [EO 4]

- Infrastructure limitations.
- Financial constraints.
- Lack of expertise.

118.   What are the top challenges to using big data and predictive analytics? [EO 4]

- Conflicting management priorities.
- Quality and availability of data.
- Personnel limitations, including sufficient staff, training, skills and capabilities.

119.   What types of data were collected by the majority of life companies? [EO 4]

A majority of companies collected medical records and prescription drug data.

120.   What types of data are collected and used by fewer companies? [EO 4]

Far fewer companies collected data from credit scores, websites, and social media sources; however, use of those sources was predicted to grow rapidly.

121.   How might health insurers use analytics? [EO 4]

The patterns in data collected on individuals could predict their anticipated healthcare needs and costs.

122.   How might the popularity of personal fitness and smart watches be used by health insurers? [EO 4]

Data collected with the consent of the wearer might be aggregated to identify patterns and predict the likelihood of certain healthcare costs based on activity levels, habits, or type of activity.

123.   What other types of data can be analyzed to predict health care costs? [EO 4]

Socioeconomic data can also reveal patterns related to overall health, including data related to consumer spending habits, demographics, occupations, criminal records, level of education, and numerous other factors. Often, individuals knowingly provide this information – for example, by completing a survey for the insurer. Others unknowingly or unconsciously provide a wealth of collectible data — for example, by using store loyalty cards that track purchases.

124.   How does the ACA affect insurers ability to use big data and predictive analytics? [EO 4]

The Affordable Care Act and state laws significantly restrict the ability of health insurers to deny coverage or apply individual rate adjustments.

125.   How are health care insurers using data analytics to reduce or prevent claim costs? [EO 4]

Health insurers are increasingly using data analytics to help reduce (or prevent) claims costs by creating wellness programs and wellness incentives. The companies may then target those insureds to receive useful information or information on insurer-paid programs to address those problems.

126.   Beginning in 2020, what method will life insurers be required to use to estimate financial statement reserves for l term and universal life with secondary guarantees?

Effective January 1, 2020, life insurers will be required to use a principle-based reserving method (often referred to simply as "PBR") to estimate reserves reported in financial statements for term and universal life with secondary guarantees (ULSG).

127.   What is the difference in reserving between property/casualty and life insurance?

Property and casualty insurers establish reserves for losses that have already occurred. For life insurance, however, reserves are determined for insured events that will occur someday in the future.

128.   How did insurers set reserves prior to principle-based reserving?

The states required all companies to use specific mortality and morbidity tables to determine reserves.

129.   What is the assumption underlying these historical rules?

These formulas essentially assume that all insurers have the same experience with mortality and investment returns.

130.   What does principle-based reserving consider to support more accurate reserving?

- Variations in insurance company size and experience;
- Individual company concentration of business (by policy type or location of insureds);
- New and more complex product offerings (including those that permit policy owners to request changes to benefits); and
- Economic factors (such as recessions and interest rate trends).

131.   What technique is used to estimate reserves under principle-based reserving?

Principle-based reserving requires companies to determine reserves using specific principles and simulation modeling.

132.   What factors will companies consider in determining reserves?

Under principle-based reserving, companies will regularly recalculate estimated reserves based on factors such as actual company experience, product and demographic composition, and economic conditions.

133.   What precipitated the move from standard valuation methods to principle-based valuation?

The move from standard valuation methods to principle-based valuation began several years ago, when the National Association of Insurance Commissioners (NAIC) adopted the Standard Valuation Law (SVL) model.

134.   What is the purpose of the NAIC's model Standard Valuation Law (SVL)?

The SVL introduced principle-based reserving as a new method of determining policy reserves and to create more uniform life insurance reserve reporting requirements among the states.

135.   List the stated goals of the Valuation Manual.

- To consolidate into one document the minimum reserve requirements for life insurance, accident and health insurance, and deposit-type contracts pursuant to the Standard Valuation Law, including those products subject to principle-based valuation requirements and those not subject to principle-based valuation requirements.
- To promote uniformity among states' valuation requirements.
- To provide for an efficient, consistent and timely process to update valuation requirements as the need arises.
- To mandate and facilitate the specific reporting requirements of experience data.
- To enhance industry compliance with the 2009 Standard Valuation Law and subsequent revisions, as adopted in various states.

136.   Which sections of the Valuation Manual focus on Experience Reporting Requirements?

Sections VM-50 and VM-51 of the Valuation Manual focus on Experience Reporting Requirements.

137.   How does the Experience Reporting Requirements' uniform reporting structure assist with the move to principle-based reserving ?

A uniform reporting structure is intended to facilitate the establishment of industry benchmarks, allow regulators to measure the reasonableness of assumptions made by companies, and facilitate any necessary future updates to the Valuation Manual.

138.   What is the purpose of Section VM-50?

Section VM-50 defines the roles of the companies, regulators, and statistical agents in the process, the intended use of the data reported, and addresses confidentiality of that data.

139.   What additional changes does the Experience Reporting Requirements call for?

- The Experience Reporting Requirements will require life insurers to report data to a statistical agent for aggregate reporting to state regulators for annual and other periodic data calls.
- The Experience Reporting Requirements place standards for data quality on both the statistical agent and the company.

140.   What is the purpose of Section VM-51?

Section VM 51 covers the required formats, including specific data elements required, for experience reporting.

141.   What changes will principle-based reserving require of life insurance data managers?

- Life insurance companies are required to process and retain more data than that required for formulaic statutory reserving methods.
- Interaction and coordination among many different departments in planning and implementing the revised methods.

142.   If life insurers offer products to which principle-based rules do not apply, what may they need to do?

Companies may have to maintain the traditional reserving method if they offer products for which principle-based reserving doesn't yet apply, such as other types of life insurance policies, health insurance, and certain annuities.

143.   What are the challenges to data managers in a life company as principle-based reserving is implemented?

Under the Experience Reporting Requirements, companies must report life insurance data at the policy level, which may require collecting additional data or coding data elements that were not previously tracked. Companies will also be required to cooperate with a statistical advisory organization and to comply with testing and error correction schedules. Data managers may find themselves steering significant departmental changes to ensure that resources are available for compliance.

144.   Identify some of the conditions that result in unclaimed benefits from life insurance policies.

- For whole life policies or those where coverage is paid up, the policy owner may not even remember that the coverage exists.

- Beneficiaries may not be aware that they are named as such —for example, an adult may forget that their elderly parent had a life insurance policy, or may never have been made aware of the policy's existence.
- Beneficiaries may know that a policy existed but be unable to locate the actual contract or remember the name of the company.
- Sometimes, the insurance company goes out of business or is acquired by another, and beneficiaries may assume that an old policy is no longer valid.

145.   How have states addressed the issue of unclaimed benefits?

Over half of the states have addressed this issue by adopting legislation based on the National Conference of Insurance Legislators (NCOIL) model Unclaimed Life Insurance Act.

146.   What does NCOIL's model Unclaimed Life Insurance Act require?

NCOIL's model bill requires companies to compare policies against the Social Security Administration's Death Master File (DMF)at least twice annually – initially against the entire DMF database, with subsequent comparisons using updates to the DMF. If the insurer finds evidence that an insured, annuity owner, or other account holder has died, the insurer must make a good-faith effort to locate beneficiaries and assist them with the claims process. The NCOIL model also requires insurers to annually report data on unclaimed benefits to the state insurance regulator.

147.   What information does the Social Security Administration's Death Master File (DMF) include?

The Social Security Administration's Death Master File (DMF) includes more than 83 million records of deaths that have been reported to the Social Security Administration, including the decedent's name, date of birth, social security number, and date of death.

148.   The NCOIL Model Act includes a requirement that insurers implement "fuzzy match" criteria that may be challenging for some companies. List the conditions that insurer's search procedures must consider.

- Common nicknames.
- Initials instead of full name.
- Middle name.
- Interchangeable first and last names.
- Partial social security numbers.
- Transposition of birth month and date or incomplete dates.
- Compound last names.

- Maiden or married names.
- Hyphens and spaces in names.

149. **Identify organizations that support the business of life and health insurers.**

- LOMA.
- LIMRA.
- American Council of Life Insurers (ACLI).
- National Alliance of Life Companies (NALC).
- National Association of Health Underwriters (NAHU).

150. **Which of these organizations are trade organizations?**

- LOMA.
- LIMRA.
- American Council of Life Insurers (ACLI).
- National Alliance of Life Companies (NALC).

151. **How does LOMA support the life insurance industry?**

LOMA administers training and education programs for insurers. LOMA also provides benchmarking information on customer service to its insurance and financial services company members.

152. **What is the Fellow Life Management Institute (FMLI) designation?**

The Fellow Life Management Institute (FMLI) designation consisting of a rigorous series of courses related to the business and operation of life insurance.

153. **How does LIMRA support the life insurance industry?**

LIMRA provides members with research and market insight to support business strategies, including product, growth, and marketing goals.

154. **What is LL Global, Inc.?**

LOMA and LIMRA merged in 2008 under parent organization, LL Global, Inc., but continue to maintain separate identities and focus.

155.   **Identify the types of coverage provided by member companies of the American Council of Life Insurers (ACLI).**

The American Council of Life Insurers (ACLI) is a national trade association of companies that offer one or more of the following: life insurance, annuities, retirement plans, long-term care and disability income insurance, and reinsurance.

156.   **How does ACLI support the life insurance industry?**

The ACLI is an advocacy organization that represents the interests of its member companies in state, federal, and international public policy issues (e.g., pending bills in the states or in Congress). The ACLI also publishes information and data for use by consumers, companies, media, and regulators.

157.   **What types of companies are served by the National Alliance of Life Companies (NALC)?**

The National Alliance of Life Companies (NALC) is a trade association formed to serve the interests of small to mid-sized companies, including health writers.

158.   **How does the NALC support its member companies?**

The NALC is an advocacy organization that represents members in matters of public policy.

159.   **Why was the NALC created?**

The NALC was created to ensure that smaller companies, which may lack the resources and infrastructure of larger companies, have a voice in legislative and regulatory issues that might affect their businesses. Data calls are an example of regulatory requirements that may be disproportionately burdensome to smaller companies compared to large companies.

160.   **Who is represented by the National Association of Health Underwriters (NAHU)?**

The National Association of Health Underwriters (NAHU)represents health insurance agents, brokers, and employee benefit professionals.

161.   **How does the National Association of Health Underwriters (NAHU) support its members?**

The NAHU advocates for members in state and federal public policy issues and provides extensive educational and networking opportunities.

162. Identify the organizations that rely on voluntarily reported data from life and health insurance companies.

- America's Health Insurance Plans (AHIP).
- Medical Information Bureau Group, Inc (MIB).

163. How is data from these organizations used?

The data is aggregated and used for various purposes to support member companies.

164. Identify America's Health Insurance Plans (AHIP)

America's Health Insurance Plans (AHIP) is a national trade association established to represent the interests of health insurers writing group benefits.

165. Identify the entities that can join America's Health Insurance Plans (AHIP).

In addition to health insurance companies, AHIP members include health care consultants, attorneys, insurance agents and brokers, practitioners, and educators.

166. What types of data are collected by AHIP from its members?

The AHIP collects premium and claim data by:

- Type of plan, deductibles rates offered, benefits, coinsurance, and copayments.
- Age, state, income, race/ethnicity, education, and urban or rural location of insureds.
- Number of applicants and number of applicants denied coverage.
- Size of groups.
- Treatment.

167. What is the focus of the Medical Information Bureau (MIB)?

The Medical Information Bureau (MIB) focuses on preventing fraud.

168. How does the Medical Information Bureau (MIB) differ from other major life and health insurance organizations?

The MIB is considered a consumer reporting agency and, like credit reporting agencies, individuals may request a copy of their personal MIB report at no charge annually.

169.   Who are MIB's members?

MIB members include hundreds of life, health, disability income, critical illness, and long-term care insurers writing in the U.S. and Canada.

170.   What information services does MIB offer its members?

The MIB collects limited information on individuals who apply for insurance through one of MIB's member companies. The MIB provides a mechanism for information exchange among members to aid underwriting and reduce fraud. Members voluntarily report information relevant to their insureds (such as admitted hazardous hobbies). When reviewing applications for new coverage, members can then access the MIB database to determine if an applicant's prior insurance carrier reported information that is not disclosed on the pending application.

171.   What function does the Life Statistical Services (LSS) serve to members?

Life Statistical Services (LSS) is a division under the MIB that functions as a statistical reporting agency. LSS is the statistical agent appointed by those states testing life insurance reporting required by principle-based reserving.